SHAAN SAHOTA

Shaan Sahota is a writer and doctor from Southall. She studied History and Modern Languages at the University of Oxford, before moving on to study medicine at the University of Cambridge. *The Estate* is Shaan's first play. It was shortlisted for the 2020 Women's Prize in Playwriting and then developed during her residency with the National Theatre Studio.

Other Titles in this Series

Waleed Akhtar
THE ART OF ILLUSION *after* Alexis Michalik
KABUL GOES POP: MUSIC TELEVISION
    AFGHANISTAN
THE P WORD
THE REAL ONES

Chris Bush
THE ASSASSINATION OF KATIE HOPKINS
    with Matt Winkworth
THE CHANGING ROOM
CHRIS BUSH PLAYS: ONE
A DOLL'S HOUSE *after* Ibsen
FAUSTUS: THAT DAMNED WOMAN
HUNGRY
JANE EYRE *after* Brontë
THE LAST NOËL
OTHERLAND
ROBIN HOOD AND THE
    CHRISTMAS HEIST
    with Matt Winkworth
ROCK / PAPER / SCISSORS
STANDING AT THE SKY'S EDGE
    with Richard Hawley
STEEL

Jez Butterworth
THE FERRYMAN
THE HILLS OF CALIFORNIA
JERUSALEM
JEZ BUTTERWORTH PLAYS: ONE
JEZ BUTTERWORTH PLAYS: TWO
MOJO
THE NIGHT HERON
PARLOUR SONG
THE RIVER
THE WINTERLING

Anupama Chandrasekhar
DISCONNECT
THE FATHER AND THE ASSASSIN
FREE OUTGOING
WHEN THE CROWS VISIT

Caryl Churchill
BLUE HEART
CHURCHILL PLAYS: THREE
CHURCHILL PLAYS: FOUR
CHURCHILL PLAYS: FIVE
CHURCHILL: SHORTS
CLOUD NINE
DING DONG THE WICKED
A DREAM PLAY *after* Strindberg
DRUNK ENOUGH TO SAY I LOVE YOU?
ESCAPED ALONE
FAR AWAY
GLASS. KILL. BLUEBEARD'S FRIENDS.
    IMP.
HERE WE GO
HOTEL
ICECREAM
LIGHT SHINING IN BUCKINGHAMSHIRE
LOVE AND INFORMATION
MAD FOREST
A NUMBER
PIGS AND DOGS
SEVEN JEWISH CHILDREN
THE SKRIKER
THIS IS A CHAIR
THYESTES *after* Seneca
TRAPS
WHAT IF IF ONLY

Natasha Gordon
NINE NIGHT

Lucy Kirkwood
BEAUTY AND THE BEAST
    with Katie Mitchell
BLOODY WIMMIN
THE CHILDREN
CHIMERICA
HEDDA *after* Ibsen
THE HUMAN BODY
IT FELT EMPTY WHEN THE HEART
    WENT AT FIRST BUT IT IS
    ALRIGHT NOW
LUCY KIRKWOOD PLAYS: ONE
MOSQUITOES
NSFW
RAPTURE
TINDERBOX
THE WELKIN

Benedict Lombe
LAVA
SHIFTERS

Winsome Pinnock
LEAVE TAKING
PIG HEART BOY *after* Malorie Blackman
ROCKETS AND BLUE LIGHTS
TAKEN
TITUBA

Mark Rosenblatt
GIANT

Jack Thorne
2ND MAY 1997
AFTER LIFE *after* Hirokazu Kore-eda
BUNNY
BURYING YOUR BROTHER IN
    THE PAVEMENT
A CHRISTMAS CAROL *after* Dickens
THE END OF HISTORY…
HOPE
JACK THORNE PLAYS: ONE
JACK THORNE PLAYS: TWO
JUNKYARD
LET THE RIGHT ONE IN
    after John Ajvide Lindqvist
THE MOTIVE AND THE CUE
MYDIDAE
THE SOLID LIFE OF SUGAR WATER
STACY & FANNY AND FAGGOT
WHEN WINSTON WENT TO WAR WITH
    THE WIRELESS
WHEN YOU CURE ME
WOYZECK *after* Büchner

debbie tucker green
BORN BAD
DEBBIE TUCKER GREEN PLAYS: ONE
DIRTY BUTTERFLY
EAR FOR EYE
HANG
NUT
A PROFOUNDLY AFFECTIONATE,
    PASSIONATE DEVOTION TO
    SOMEONE (– *NOUN*)
RANDOM
STONING MARY
TRADE & GENERATIONS
TRUTH AND RECONCILIATION

Shaan Sahota

THE ESTATE

NICK HERN BOOKS
London
www.nickhernbooks.co.uk

A Nick Hern Book

The Estate first published in Great Britain in 2025 as a paperback original by Nick Hern Books Limited, The Glasshouse, 49a Goldhawk Road, London W12 8QP

The Estate copyright © 2025 Shaan Sahota

Shaan Sahota has asserted her right to be identified as the author of this work

Cover image: Photography of Adeel Akhtar by Gavin Li; Art direction and design by National Theatre Graphic Design Studio

Designed and typeset by Nick Hern Books, London
Printed in Great Britain by Mimeo Ltd, Huntingdon, Cambridgeshire PE29 6XX

A CIP catalogue record for this book is available from the British Library

ISBN 978 1 83904 444 1

CAUTION All rights whatsoever in this play are strictly reserved. Requests to reproduce the text in whole or in part should be addressed to the publisher. This book may not be used, in whole or in part, for the development or training of artificial intelligence technologies or systems.

Amateur Performing Rights Applications for performance, including readings and excerpts, by amateurs in the English language throughout the world should be addressed to the Performing Rights Manager, Nick Hern Books, The Glasshouse, 49a Goldhawk Road, London W12 8QP, *tel* +44 (0)20 8749 4953, *email* rights@nickhernbooks.co.uk, except as follows:

Australia: ORiGiN Theatrical, *email* enquiries@originmusic.com.au, *web* www.origintheatrical.com.au

New Zealand: Play Bureau, 20 Rua Street, Mangapapa, Gisborne, 4010, *tel* +64 21 258 3998, *email* info@playbureau.com

United States of America and Canada: Curtis Brown Ltd, see details below.

Professional Performing Rights Application for performance by professionals in any medium and in any language throughout the world should be addressed to Curtis Brown Ltd, Cunard House, 15 Regent Street, St. James's, London SW1Y 4LR, *tel* +44 (0)20 7393 4400, *fax* +44 (0)20 7393 4401, *email* cb@curtisbrown.co.uk

No performance of any kind may be given unless a licence has been obtained. Applications should be made before rehearsals begin. Publication of this play does not necessarily indicate its availability for amateur performance.

www.nickhernbooks.co.uk/environmental-policy

Nick Hern Books' authorised representative in the EU is
Easy Access System Europe – Mustamäe tee 50, 10621 Tallinn, Estonia
email gpsr.requests@easproject.com

The Estate was first performed in the Dorfman auditorium of the National Theatre, London, on 17 July 2025 (previews from 9 July), with the following cast:

ANGAD	Adeel Akhtar
MALICKA	Shelley Conn
SANGEETA	Dinita Gohil
GYAN	Thusitha Jayasundera
RALPH	Humphrey Ker
ISAAC	Fode Simbo
PETRA	Helena Wilson
VOICE OF PETER LONG	Richard Goulding

With the voices of Patrick Marber and Anjana Vasan

MUSICIANS
Ranjit Singh
Sewa Singh
Surinder Singh

Musicians coordinated by Dr Onkar S Sahota MBA FRCGP
Recorded at the National Theatre and engineered by
Niall John Acott

Director	Daniel Raggett
Set Designer	Chloe Lamford
Costume Designer	Khadija Raza
Lighting Designer	Jessica Hung Han Yun
Composer	Asaf Zohar
Sound Designer	Mike Winship
Movement Director	Polly Bennett
Fight Director	Alex Payne
Casting	Bryony Jarvis-Taylor CDG
Voice Coach	Shereen Ibrahim
Staff Director	Molly Stacey

*For my father and my mother
who sounded like giants,
even when they didn't mean to.*

Characters

ANGAD SINGH (*Harrow; New College, Oxford*), *MP for Reading and Shadow Secretary of State for Environment, Food and Rural Affairs*
PETRA (*Wycombe Abbey; Magdalen, Oxford*), *Communications Special Advisor in Angad's office*
ISAAC (*Alma Mater unknown; Diversity Access Scheme*), *Angad's Policy Assistant*
RALPH HUGHES (*rowing captain at Harrow; Merton, Oxford*), *Opposition Chief Whip in the House of Commons*
GYAN (*Langley Grammar; Sheffield Medical School*), *Angad's sister*
SANGEETA (*St Paul's Girls'; Jesus, Oxford*), *Angad's wife*
MALICKA (*Langley Grammar; University College London*), *ended up in California, Angad's sister*
VOICE OF PETER LONG (*debate captain at Eton; Oriel, Oxford*), *outgoing Leader of His Majesty's Opposition*
NEWS, *voice-over*

Note on Text

A forward slash (/) indicates when the next line is spoken.

This text went to press before the end of rehearsals and so may differ slightly from the play as performed.

ACT ONE

Scene One – The Party Office

Office of Angad Singh.

The office is a flurry of activity. Pages of paper pour out of the printer: the party machinery is gearing up, as members prepare for a leadership contest.

PETRA *pursues* ANGAD, *brandishing a pot of concealer.*

ANGAD. Get that away from me.

PETRA. You're supposed to go two shades lighter for concealer.

ANGAD. I'm not launching my campaign in whiteface.

PETRA. Listen to me, Angad, you don't have a choice. Dark circles make a man look extremely untrustworthy.

ANGAD. Don't they show I've been up late, working hard?

PETRA. Unelectable.

PETRA*'s phone dings. She reads the headline.*

He's resigning. It's streaming now.

ANGAD. Get it up.

They huddle around PETRA*'s laptop where Peter Long's resignation speech plays out.*

LONG (*voice-over*).…heavy heart that I announce my resignation / from my role as leader of His Majesty's opposition. It has been the privilege of my life to serve this party and to fight for the nation's best interest from the benches of the opposition. But I have decided to step down from politics to spend more time with my wife and our two children, and it is for their sake that I ask for privacy at this time.

PETRA (*pointing at the screen*). Wife?

ANGAD (*nods*). She's going to castrate him.

PETRA. It'll be good for him.

Pause as they listen.

No, it's too much. He's milking it.

I think it might be tear stick.

ANGAD. The man is going to be castrated, he's allowed to be moved.

PETRA. He's not crying they're just leaking out.

ANGAD peers closer.

ANGAD. Tear sticks in British politics, we really are in crisis. What happened to the stiff upper lip?

PETRA. New. Labour.

PETRA slams the laptop.

At least she was eighteen.

ANGAD. Exactly. He'll be alright.

PETRA's phone dings: a message.

PETRA. David Shah, wants to know if you're running.

ANGAD. Would he back me?

PETRA. Hard to say. Might be running himself. (*She reads aloud as she replies.*) 'Angad is stunned...'

ANGAD. And worried about Peter's family –

Enter ISAAC, carrying three coffees.

PETRA (*nodding*)....and v v worried about Peter's family... Nothing could be further from his mind.'

ISAAC. Brent East. Eyebrow guy. Wants to know if you're running.

ANGAD. What did you say?

ISAAC. I said there was more chance of you being reincarnated as a satsuma.

PETRA. Isaac –

ISAAC. What? Doesn't sound too ambitious. But at the same time I didn't say no, keeping the door open. It's perfect. Anyway – (*He checks no one can hear.*) he said you could count on his support.

PETRA. Ooh I love contest season. He has good donor connections.

ANGAD. He retweeted me on carers' visas.

ISAAC. People like your policies, boss.

PETRA. No one is reading your policies, Angad, it's you. Our voters want to believe they live in a country where the son of a baggage handler can rise to the top. The party knows that.

ISAAC. It's a good story.

ANGAD. It's my story.

ISAAC. Did you guys see Long's resignation? He looked so sad.

PETRA*'s mobile rings.*

PETRA. Grow up. Angad Singh's office. Speaking? Oh hello, darling… (*Mouths to* ANGAD.) *Times*.

I mean, he's completely stunned. Mm…

I know, she looks terrible, I thought it was his mother!… Mmm…

What? Nothing could be further from his mind.

ISAAC *glances down the corridor as he hangs up his coat.*

ISAAC. Ralph Hughes, incoming.

PETRA (*mouthing*). Shit.

PETRA *steps behind the internal office divide to continue her call in the next room.* ANGAD *sees an inhaler on his desk and shoves it in his drawer like it's a dirty magazine.*

RALPH HUGHES *enters. He lingers in the doorway, on his phone.*

ANGAD. An unannounced visit from the Whip, am I in trouble?

Beat.

RALPH. Mmm. Who are you backing?

ANGAD. I hadn't thought about it.

To be honest, I'm just stunned.

I didn't see Long's resignation coming. It's such a shame.

RALPH. Mmm.

ANGAD. Tobias said it was actually him. He tweeted the picture himself?

RALPH *smiles at a gif he's received.*

RALPH. I think he'd had a heavy night. It was the Christ Church gaudy.

ANGAD. The Christ Church lot always take it too far. I had to throw away my shirt after my first time I went to a Christ formal.

RALPH. I said that to him, I told him 'I'm not saying you can't partake, but you need to learn your limits.'

ANGAD. That's good advice.

RALPH *finally puts his phone away.*

RALPH. It's excellent advice, but nonetheless, he has fucked us in the collective arsehole with a cautionary tale for the ages. I'd shoot him if I wasn't sure his wife's punishment was going to be more excruciating than anything I could imagine. Did you know her?

ANGAD *shakes his head.*

Brasenose. She was a virgin when she graduated, she'll have his balls for this. Anyway, at least she was eighteen.

ANGAD. Exactly, he'll be fine.

RALPH. Look I'm just stopping by but I've been surveying the land, and really, nobody wants a contest. Not the voters, not the donors, not the members. I think everyone agrees that what the party really needs is unity. What do you think?

ANGAD. Well certainly, I agree unity is absolutely paramount.

RALPH. We don't need dick-swinging, theatrics and front-stabbing.

ANGAD. No.

RALPH. We're a year out from the election, changing our leader now will hurt the party but a contest could destroy us.

PETRA *re-enters the room.*

PETRA. You want an anointment?

RALPH. An anointment. Yup. The party puts one candidate to the members. We avoid all the division and ugliness of another contest. Poking at old wounds which haven't quite healed from the last one. What do you say?

ANGAD. I don't know. It feels a little... Callicles.

RALPH. Well, precisely. Callicles does win.

They both laugh.

ISAAC. Who are you saying you want to anoint?

RALPH. Well, Dobson seems like the obvious choice.

ANGAD. Edward Dobson?

RALPH. He's already had forty offers to nominate him. He has experience in government, the Cabinet trusts him. Who else?

ANGAD. Edward Dobson? I don't know.

ISAAC. I mean, he looks just like the last guy.

PETRA. Looks like him, sounds like him. I think they have the same godfather.

RALPH. You want to know why we lost the last election? People felt they couldn't trust us. How do we show our voters they can trust us if we walk into the election, fresh from a contest stabbing each other in the neck? Trust me, an anointment is our only chance.

ANGAD. Or maybe we could show them we've changed?

RALPH. Don't be so dramatic.

ANGAD looks at PETRA. She nods.

ANGAD. More than that, I think things actually need to change.

RALPH fires off a quick email as ANGAD speaks.

I had to take my dad to the hospital last week. He waited six hours for an ambulance and none came. Six hours not knowing if he was in serious danger, six hours too scared to go to the toilet. And when we go there, it was a total nightmare, people were holding bowls of their own vomit and there were nurses crying in every half-quiet corner.

And at that very moment our party leader was, well the whole country knows what our leader was doing and it's not good enough. I kept thinking – 'I have to do something.'

Beat. As everyone waits for RALPH to finish his email.

RALPH. One second... Yes. Sorry that your father's not been right. How is he now?

ANGAD. He's alright, yeah, thanks. Should be coming home today.

RALPH. Good. Still driving that enormous Jaguar?

ANGAD nods. RALPH chuckles.

ANGAD. I have to do something. You understand that, don't you?

RALPH. You want to do something? This is doing something.

Declare for Dobson, and you can get your agenda onto a winning manifesto. I'll have you on *Question Time* this Thursday telling that... hospital story to the country. I'll even get you a main slot at the party conference. Yes? Happy? Can I assure Edward he has your support?

ISAAC. You know I've heard people want a contest.

RALPH. Where have you heard that?

ISAAC. I can't remember.

RALPH. Try. Because I've got pledges from half the Shadow Cabinet to support Dobson, so anyone who pushes for a contest now is going to find himself in an extremely lonely little spot.

ISAAC. Cool cool... yeah... I'll pass that on to him.

PETRA. Hypothetically, if Angad were to declare for Dobson for the good of the party, how might Dobson reward that?

RALPH *looks at* PETRA, *irritated*.

Petra Wallace. Comms.

RALPH. Well. The member who does what's best for the party is someone we'd like to see rise to great things.

PETRA. We'd need something more specific than that because. Well. Angad's actually been receiving a steady stream of calls, urging him to run. For the good of the party.

RALPH. For the good of the party?

PETRA *looks to* ANGAD *to speak*.

ANGAD. Our voters want to believe they live in a country where the son of a baggage handler can rise to the top job of that country. Maybe that could help turn our image around? People need to believe that things could get better for them.

RALPH. I'm sorry, who's the baggage handler?

ANGAD. What? My dad.

ANGAD *points to himself, half apologetically*.

RALPH. I thought your father was in business.

ANGAD. He got his first shop the year before I joined Harrow. Before that it was bags, buses, toilets. Anything.

RALPH. Were you thinking of running?

ANGAD. I could. For the good of the party.

RALPH. I remember you sitting out from games absolutely shivering in your shorts at the height of June. And now look at you sticking your head right into the scrum, playing rough with the Firsts.

RALPH *turns his back on* PETRA, *cutting her out of the conversation.*

No one becomes party leader from Rural Affairs, Gadsy. It just doesn't happen. Between you and me, if you were to declare your support for Dobson, for the good of the party, I think people would really take notice.

ANGAD. You think they'd notice me for not running?

PETRA *laughs. This annoys* RALPH.

RALPH. Yes. I think they would. Now. Can I tell Edward you have no intention of running and he has your support.

ANGAD *nods.* RALPH *slaps him on the back.*

Good man. It's the right thing to do.

(*To* ISAAC *and* PETRA.) By the way, this is all –

He makes a gesture to suggest 'off the record'.

RALPH *leaves.*

PETRA. Holy shit that man just reeks of power, I can still smell it in the air.

PETRA *wafts the air towards herself, relishing the smell.* ANGAD *skulks into a corner, licking his wounds.*

ISAAC. I think we should burn sage.

ANGAD. Did he seem annoyed at me?

ISAAC. Angad, why didn't you tell us your dad's in hospital?

ANGAD. Oh. It was indigestion in the end. He's one of those old Indian men who'd rather call an ambulance than wait for his GP to call him back.

ACT ONE, SCENE ONE   17

PETRA. Well, I think you did the right thing. Ralph Hughes's candidate has won the last four contests and yup. It makes a lot of sense to back Dobson.

ISAAC. And speaking at the conference is a really big deal. Well done on negotiating that one, boss.

ANGAD. Yeah... yeah... Maybe I could play for Shadow Home Secretary if Dobson wins. What do you think?

ISAAC. I can see that. Very strong.

Beat.

PETRA. It's funny he's going for Dobson. Right after we've had one perve resign.

ISAAC. What do you mean?

PETRA. Well, Dobson's got the... the whole thing for –

She makes a sexually depraved gesture, suggestive of tickling.

ANGAD. You know about that?

PETRA. Ohmygod do you know?

ANGAD. He was in my college. I thought... I assumed he'd grown out of it.

The office phone rings. ISAAC *answers it.*

ISAAC. It's security, your sister is downstairs.

ANGAD. My sister?

ISAAC. Can they send her up?

ANGAD. Yeah. Sure.

PETRA. My godmother was at school with Dobson's wife. Not grown out of it.

ISAAC. Can someone please tell me what we're talking about?

PETRA. Dobson's wife told my godmother who told Mummy that Dobson's a real perve for tickling. But forget what you know about tickling. He needs to be on top, pinning you down, all red-faced. And you have to scream, like you're really struggling, 'No, no, please stop, PLEASE!'

ISAAC. What is wrong with this party?

ANGAD *picks his phone up from his jacket pocket and frowns.*

ANGAD. My sister left me ten missed calls.

PETRA. What was the word?

…

MERCY. That's it. You have to say 'I'm begging you. MERCY.'

ISAAC. You're telling me our boy Dobson's a freak.

PETRA. He got caught watching some pretty hardcore stuff on the Commons Wi-Fi a few years back, but they dealt with it internally. It's the only thing that gets his dick hard.

ANGAD. Petra, enough!

I just pledged my support for Dobson, I could be his Shadow Home Secretary and you're here, spouting ancient rumours about him.

PETRA. Oh I see.

ANGAD. It's not acceptable, no. It demeans you. It demeans us.

PETRA. You're right, Angad, I'm sorry about that. That was undignified of me. Discretion, thy name is a comms manager.

GYAN JOHAR, *Angad's sister, enters, looking frazzled.*

ANGAD. What are you doing here?

GYAN. I've been trying to get through for two hours.

ANGAD. Is / everything okay?

GYAN. I need a way to get hold of you in an emergency, you can't just disappear, I need to be able to contact you.

ANGAD. I'm sorry, it's been really crazy today. Peter resigned. Is everything okay?

ACT ONE, SCENE ONE 19

GYAN. No. It's not. I just came from the hospital.

Beat.

ANGAD. Is it Dad?

Beat.

Is he okay?

GYAN. I'm really sorry, Splinty.

ANGAD. Has he… He's died, hasn't he. Has he?

GYAN *nods.* ANGAD *steadies himself. Beat.*

ISAAC. I am so so / sorry.

ANGAD. Guys, could you give us a minute?

ISAAC. Course, boss.

ISAAC *and* PETRA *hurry out.*

ANGAD. I thought he was fine.

GYAN. I know.

ANGAD. I thought he was coming home.

GYAN. I thought so too.

ANGAD. What happened?

GYAN. I think it was his heart all along.

ANGAD. Fuck.

What happened? Was he in pain?

GYAN. I don't know what to say. I think he was really, really brave.

ANGAD. Have you told Malicka?

GYAN. Not yet.

ANGAD. She's going to be pissed. She asked me if she should fly over and I said, 'Nah, don't bother, he's fine.' I'm such a fucking idiot.

GYAN. Angad, stop it.

ANGAD. I told him to stop calling the ambulance.

GYAN. Don't be like that.

ANGAD covers his face.

ANGAD. I'm an idiot.

Beat.

GYAN. Do you remember last year, when he called you to pick him up from the police station?

The tenants at twenty-eight said Dad held an electric drill to their head when they didn't have the rent. Said he threatened to beat them up with a hoover.

Do you remember what Dad said?

ANGAD. He said he was seventy-eight, with a triple bypass. That the guys were making it up because they didn't want to get evicted.

GYAN. That's right. And the police believed him.

ANGAD. Never explained the black eye though, did he.

GYAN. Dad was a really tough cookie.

ANGAD. You never knew if you could believe him.

GYAN. 'You never knew if you could believe him.' You didn't mess up here.

Beat.

Imagine having him as your landlord and not paying your rent.

ANGAD. A hoover, Dad.

GYAN smiles. ANGAD groans.

I should've been with him. I didn't realise this was it, what am I doing?

GYAN. Angad, no. He was so proud of you, he wanted you out here fighting.

ANGAD. He didn't even see me do anything.

GYAN. He told every nurse and cleaner in that hospital about you.

ANGAD. I needed more time. I wanted to show him that breaking his back meant something. He didn't even get to meet my baby!

GYAN *comforts* ANGAD *with a mothering gesture.*

GYAN. The day you were born, he was in such a foul mood. He was so scared you would be another girl, he had this explosive diarrhoea all day. And then it was you, and he was just so happy. Don't forget that. Just by being born you made him so happy.

Beat.

ANGAD. Thanks, Splinty.

GYAN. You're getting a bald patch.

ANGAD. Okay. I'll put out a notice in the *Des Pardes* and *Punjab Times*.

GYAN. Good.

ANGAD. Let's find out how soon Malicka can get here. Then we should fix a date for the funeral.

GYAN. I'm right behind you.

ANGAD. Let's give him a good send-off.

Scene Two – The Gurdwara

PETRA *and* ISAAC *stand in the langar hall of Southall Gurdwara sipping masala chai. They can see people entering the temple and the prayer hall from their vantage point. Kirtan (funerary hymns accompanied by a harmonium and tabla) play out through the speakers*

ISAAC. It's like a state funeral...

PETRA. The state of Punjab, maybe.

ISAAC. Do you know what he did?

PETRA. I think you would call him a Corner-Shop Mughal. Side notes of slum landlord. Angad's always been a little slippery on the details. I wasn't expecting open casket, I have to say.

ISAAC. Angad looked like a little kid when he was carrying the body.

PETRA. Are you kidding. He's aged ten years. His dark circles have gone from here to here –

She points from her cheekbones to her jaw.

Who's that he's talking to?

ISAAC. That is Mr Cheema, president of the gurdwara.

PETRA. What's he doing, what's that laugh? I've never seen that laugh.

ISAAC. Angad knows what he's doing. If it comes to a General Election, Mr Cheema could get out enough votes to swing this borough. Maybe.

PETRA. Mr Cheema doesn't speak English.

ISAAC. He doesn't need to speak English to tell this crowd who to vote for.

The temples here sponsor visas, they organise welfare and trust me, even if you can't understand it, when they're up on the mic, they're preaching politics.

PETRA. I almost forgot you did that Masters at SOAS.

ISAAC. Little more useful than Classics at Magdalen.

PETRA. So you say.

> PETRA *grabs* ISAAC'*s arm and gestures towards the prayer hall.*
>
> Shadow Chancellor, with David Shah.

ISAAC. What the hell – that's six members of the Shadow Cabinet in Southall on a Tuesday morning.

PETRA. I think I've seen thirty backbenchers.

ISAAC. Do you think it's a signal? To show they would back Angad?

PETRA. Well, I don't think they're in the gurdwara because they're interested in converting, if that's what you're suggesting

ISAAC. I knew it, I knew people wanted a contest.

PETRA. Dobson's turnout's been pretty anaemic. Trod on too many toes on the way up.

ISAAC. Angad's looking like a fresh new face.

PETRA. He was good on *QT*.

ISAAC. He killed it! He was clear, he was funny. He's looking like change and yeah, I'll say it. A good guy. Makes me feel kinda hopeful.

> PETRA *rolls her eyes.* ANGAD *joins* PETRA *and* ISAAC.
>
> How are you holding up, boss? It's been a very lovely service.

ANGAD. I haven't really had a minute, yeah, I think it's good to stay busy. Have you guys eaten?

ISAAC. Where's Sangeeta, I haven't seen her.

ANGAD. Pregnant women aren't supposed to see the body. She's on her way now.

PETRA. I have to say this is the best attended funeral I've ever been to. Did all these people know your father?

ANGAD. My dad ran his shops on these streets for thirty years. He was the man who sold them mangoes and made them masala chai when they got off the plane in a cold new country.

ISAAC. That's really beautiful.

Thanks for having us, Angad, it felt really spiritual, and special.

PETRA. You couldn't understand a word of it.

ISAAC. Music can move you and you don't have to know why.

PETRA. Jesus Christ, are you sure you're cut out for politics? Angad, I couldn't help but notice that a surprising number of the Shadow Cabinet are in attendance.

ISSAC. Maybe they want a real leadership contest, / boss.

ANGAD. Please. I do not want to talk about politics at my father's funeral.

Beat.

But yes I did notice.

I ran into the party chairman coming out of the toilet, he asked me if I'm running.

He looks around to see who's listening.

Paul Clementine told me I could count on his support.

ISAAC. You're joking.

PETRA. He'd bring fifty backbenchers with him. Easy.

ISAAC. What the actual fuck is happening!

PETRA. Isaac, please, not in a gurdwara.

ISAAC. I am so sorry.

PETRA. Well think about it, Dobson's been polling badly with the public. Angad knocks it out the park on *QT*.

ANGAD. I think I did alright.

PETRA. You were phenomenal.

ANGAD. People said I came off like a natural statesman.

PETRA *gestures to 'concealer over dark circles'*.

PETRA. You looked rested. Like a face the party wants to put forward, well here they are. Are you speaking today?

ANGAD. Yeah, I'll get going when Sangeeta arrives.

PETRA. You have a sitting audience of major party players, no questions, no rebuttals. It could be the perfect moment to launch. Unofficially.

ANGAD. Petra, this is my father's funeral.

PETRA (*touches his arm*). And it's full of Westminster big boys.

Enter SANGEETA, *Angad's wife. She inserts herself between* PETRA *and* ANGAD.

Sangeeta! Love the scarf.

SANGEETA. Can I have a moment with my husband?

ANGAD. Alright, team. I'll catch up with you later.

PETRA *and* ISAAC *walk away to another table, with their masala chai.*

SANGEETA. How was it?

ANGAD. It was good to see the body. I was dreading it but it was good, I could see it wasn't him any more. Gyan said I should show him the *Evening Standard* write-up, like take the paper to the crematorium and I thought about it, then yeah, it wasn't him any more.

SANGEETA. Oh jaan, I'm sorry.

ANGAD. He looked so small in there. His kara used to seem so huge.

SANGEETA. I wish I was there with you.

ANGAD. Your mum's flowers were really nice.

ANGAD *rubs his face.* SANGEETA *grabs his hand.*

SANGEETA. *Don't* rub your eyes, Angad.

ANGAD. Maybe I should be running for leader.

SANGEETA. Why, what happened?

ANGAD. It's been mad here.

SANGEETA. I thought I saw, what's-his-name. Balliol, year above you. Shadow Justice.

ANGAD. Paul Clementine. He said he'd back me.

SANGEETA. Are you serious? Didn't he flush your head down the toilet in first year.

ANGAD. What's that got to do with anything? He'd bring fifty backbenchers with him if he backs me.

SANGEETA. Jaan, well done, this is incredible.

Across the doorway, they see RALPH *walk past with a Sikh handkerchief tied to his head.* PETRA *and* ISAAC *notice it too.*

ANGAD. *Fuck.*

SANGEETA. What?

ANGAD *gestures towards the doorway.*

ANGAD. Ralph Hughes has come down here to keep an eye on me.

SANGEETA. Ugh, he is such a dweeb.

ANGAD. I promised Ralph I wouldn't run and that I'd support Dobson.

SANGEETA *adjusts* ANGAD's *tie.*

SANGEETA. So what. What would your dad say?

ANGAD. Dad would say, if I didn't put it in writing then it didn't happen.

SANGEETA. Exactly. Do you think you can win now?

ANGAD. I think I could. Maybe.

SANGEETA. Then you should do it.

ANGAD. I don't know.

SANGEETA. Why not. I'm not getting any thinner, the time is now.

ANGAD. You think?

Oh my God, my chacha is wiping his hands on his beard in front of Ralph.

SANGEETA. Jaan, relax.

ANGAD. Can you go stop him?

SANGEETA. Who cares what Ralph Hughes thinks about your chacha.

ANGAD. Make sure no one from my family talks to Ralph.

SANGEETA. Sure. Okay. Did I tell you, I fingered his brother's butthole at Bryanston and I can promise you, their shit does stink.

ANGAD. What?

SANGEETA *puts a finger to* ANGAD*'s nose, he ducks away and makes a face.*

SANGEETA. I'm kidding! Come on, relax.

ANGAD*'s sisters,* GYAN *and* MALICKA, *approach to hand keys to* SANGEETA, *and give* ANGAD *the mic.*

ANGAD. I should go give my speech.

SANGEETA. Jaan, this is all really good. Enjoy it.

ANGAD. Could you go check in with Malicka and Gyan when you do matha tek.

SANGEETA. Sure. I love you.

ANGAD. I'll see you up there.

SANGEETA *leaves for the prayer hall.* ANGAD *approaches* PETRA *and* ISAAC.

You two should head up too.

> (*Rehearsing.*) My father came to this country with twelve pounds in his pocket.

PETRA. There's a lot of people here.

ANGAD. Petra.

> PETRA *discreetly offers* ANGAD *her concealer. This time he doesn't refuse it. The room has emptied. In a quiet corner, she applies it on him.*
>
> Hypothetically, what could we do with the tickling story?

PETRA. Well. We have options. Hypothetically.

> I could tell Paul's secretary? He's extremely indiscreet. It'll be all over Westminster by teatime.

ANGAD. Mmm. What else?

PETRA. Well, hypothetically we could anonymously leak it to the press. Public interest. Women's safety is still pretty hot.

ANGAD. No. No. We can't do that.

PETRA. Right. But hypothetically speaking, a man with skeletons in his closet probably shouldn't be trusted with state secrets. If I know it, every bot in cyberspace knows it. Do you think Putin wouldn't go there?

ANGAD. It's time for my speech.

PETRA. Great. Don't forget the big boys.

ANGAD (*rehearsing, to himself*). My father came to this country…

> My father can't see that half of Westminster came here for him.
>
> They're here for you.
>
> Can you see this, Dad?
>
> ANGAD *walks into the centre of the stage. All the other characters assemble to listen.* ANGAD's *voice falters with grief.*
>
> Hello. Can everyone hear me?

ACT ONE, SCENE TWO 29

Vaheguru ji ka kalsa, Vaheguru ji ke fatheh.

My father came to this country in 1978 with twelve pounds in his pocket and a belief that life could get better.

I asked him if he was afraid. He laughed and told me he'd never been afraid of anything in his life, and I think we could all see that in him. He was fearless.

He sold his ancestral land and headed for a new shore without looking back. England didn't exactly provide a warm welcome for a young man wrapped in a turban but he did find opportunity. Like many of you here, he worked in the McVities factory, at Heathrow, in shops on the Broadway. Humble work, that grew over decades and made him a pillar of the community.

I look at my father's struggle and I'm stunned. By his bravery, and the audacity of his dreams. Despite the violence he fled and the uncertainty he encountered, he always believed he could make his life better, make his children's lives better. He always believed his struggle would amount to something.

A feeling that time might have stopped for a moment.

Let me do for you, what my father did for me. Let me dream that things can be better for you. Let me work for you. Let me stay up late thinking of your troubles. Let my hands grow hard for you.

Give me the honour of serving you and let us believe together that the future we move towards can be better than the past we're escaping.

Time returns to normal. ANGAD's speech is more confident, more statesmanly.

Let me dream for you. If you let me, I will take us further and higher than ever.

(*To* PETRA.) Do it.

She smiles and sends the message, she's already primed.

Scene Three

The Singh family home, open-plan kitchen. SANGEETA *hangs laundry out to dry.* ANGAD *walks in, wearing his glasses and listening to a newsreel on his phone.*

NEWS (*voice-over*). – was the latest Cabinet member to express his doubts about Edward Dobson's suitability to lead the party and to join growing calls for an open leadership contest.

ANGAD. The committee's meeting tonight, they're going to announce an open leadership contest.

He shows SANGEETA *his phone.*

SANGEETA. That's brilliant.

ANGAD. Fifty-seven per cent approval rating from Ipsos.

Forty-eight per cent say I would make 'a very good or fairly good leader'. That's better than Dobson.

SANGEETA *continues hanging up wet clothes.*

SANGEETA. Well done.

ANGAD. Do you think I can get ten members to nominate me?

SANGEETA. Easy.

ANGAD. You think?

SANGEETA. There were twenty people in the gurdwara today ready to nominate you.

ANGAD *notices that* SANGEETA *is hanging the laundry.*

ANGAD. This is my job.

SANGEETA. It's fine.

ANGAD. Let me do it.

ANGAD *joins* SANGEETA, *and she tries not be irritated as he gets in her way.* ANGAD *knocks an item* SANGEETA *has just hung onto the floor.*

SANGEETA. Angad!

ACT ONE, SCENE THREE 31

She brushes dirt off the wet clothing.

ANGAD. Why don't you let me help you?

SANGEETA. Because it was wet in the machine for two hours and you only feel like doing it the second I am already doing it but it's okay, it's already getting done.

ANGAD. Are you annoyed at me?

SANGEETA. Why don't you do something I'm not already doing?

ANGAD. Yeah. Like what?

SANGEETA. Like what time are your sisters coming?

ANGAD. I don't know. Around eight.

SANGEETA. So what are you going to feed them?

ANGAD. There's all the food from yesterday.

SANGEETA. They won't want to eat cold pakoras from the funeral for the second time in one day.

SANGEETA *goes to the fridge and starts pulling out drink options onto the counter. Wines. Soft drinks. Two packets of crisps from a cupboard.*

They're coming at dinner time, after a funeral, to read a will. They will expect you to feed them. Why haven't you thought of this?

ANGAD. We can order pizza. Why are you getting stressed?

SANGEETA. Because I know what's going to happen.

ANGAD. What's going to happen?

SANGEETA. They are going to use this as an excuse to pick on you.

ANGAD. Can you please relax.

SANGEETA. No I can't relax because you can't sort anything.

ANGAD *comes over and rubs her shoulders.*

ANGAD. Hey can you trust me on this? It's my family. I will sort it. Let me take this off your plate.

SANGEETA. It's off my plate?

ANGAD. It's off your plate. It's on my plate.

SANGEETA. Fine.

SANGEETA pours herself a glass of wine and sits down, looking at her phone. ANGAD follows her (instantly forgetting the laundry and the hosting prep).

ANGAD. People said my speech came across very well.

SANGEETA. I can't get over how fat Dobson is.

ANGAD. Did I seem like a party leader?

SANGEETA nods, and takes a sip of wine, still looking at her phone.

SANGEETA. He is so fat he had to announce his campaign in a formal fucking sneaker.

ANGAD. Do you think people saw me in a different light?

SANGEETA. It was the perfect funeral speech –

She sips wine.

ANGAD. My father was a man who had the bravery to dream things could get better. Mr Speaker, this is a story of hope, a story of ambition, a story of grit.

SANGEETA takes another sip as she scrolls.

Do you think that's a good idea?

SANGEETA. What?

ANGAD. We want our baby to be smart. Like her mummy.

SANGEETA. Me drinking a glass of wine isn't the rate-limiting factor here. Have you forgotten, the baby is going to be related to Malicka.

She laughs then sees ANGAD's face.

I'm *kidding*!

ANGAD. I thought you two were getting on.

SANGEETA. I thought I liked her when I hadn't seen her for four years.

ANGAD. Malicka's not so bad...

SANGEETA. She's a moron, our daughter cannot be like her.

ANGAD. Any time I'm in an argument, I wish she was with me.

SANGEETA. Don't just agree with them if they get angry, okay?

ANGAD. Okay.

SANGEETA. If Gyan cries, just put a pin in the conversation. You cannot win against a crying woman.

ANGAD goes to the laundry and resumes hanging.

Just because someone is angry, or sad, it doesn't mean they're right, okay?

ANGAD. Got it.

SANGEETA. It doesn't mean you're responsible for it.

Don't let them bully you, okay.

ANGAD. Okay.

SANGEETA. Angad!

ANGAD. Yes?

SANGEETA. Don't do what they tell you to do.

ANGAD. I won't.

SANGEETA. If Malicka tries to bring up / the time when –

ANGAD. Sangeeta, give it a break

SANGEETA. Don't speak to me like that.

ANGAD. I'm sorry.

SANGEETA. There is a non-zero probability that your sisters are going to try to force you into doing something you don't want to do and I am the one person looking out for you!

The doorbell rings. He kisses her.

ANGAD. You're right. I'm sorry.

> SANGEETA *leaves to open the door. She returns with* MALICKA, *who is visibly taken by the style and scale of their home.*

MALICKA. Wow. This is so lovely.

SANGEETA. Thanks, Malicka.

> MALICKA *puts her face to the garden door, assessing the size of the garden.*

MALICKA. No wonder you're in love with your father-in-law. Sat Sri Akal Angad.

> ANGAD *gives her a side-squeeze.*

ANGAD. How's it going, Mal, how are things?

MALICKA. What can I say? My father has died and I am in mourning. Mourning, both for the father I lost and the father I never had.

> SANGEETA *catches* ANGAD*'s eye behind* MALICKA*'s back and mimes loading a rifle and violently shooting herself in the head.*

Does that make sense?

SANGEETA. It makes a lot of sense.

ANGAD. What can I get you to drink?

MALICKA. What do you have?

> ANGAD *looks at the wine that* SANGEETA *laid out, seeing it for the first time.*

ANGAD. We have red, we have white.

MALICKA. You know, to start, do you have some sparkling water?

ANGAD. Sparkling water.

SANGEETA. It's in the fridge.

ANGAD *heads to the fridge.* MALICKA*'s text alert sounds: a Buddhist gong.*

MALICKA. Gyan.

MALICKA *holds out her phone, long-sightedly, and squints.*

'Stuck in surgery. With you ASAP. Start without me.'

How can someone make that many typos in a five-word text?

ANGAD. She went to work?

MALICKA. Of course we can't start without her!

MALICKA *places a large brown envelope on the kitchen counter.*

ANGAD. I thought she was taking the day off.

MALICKA. She is a GP, for God's sake, what are these delusions of grandeur? As if she can't take a day off. As if the nation would fall to its knees. It is not a 'surgery'. It is a suburban office. Where she sits on the phone and has not seen a real patient for years so God / knows why she carries that bag of medical equipment from door to door. 'Ask me what I do for a living. Please. I beg you.'

SANGEETA *fills up her wine glass.*

SANGEETA. I think she's the only partner at the moment. They haven't been able to find one since the old dude retired.

MALICKA. Staying with her is such a nightmare. She's up till one a.m. pacing the house, her cortisol is ramped up to here.

I can hear her sighing through the walls, it's her nervous system trying to regulate. She gets home from work completely wired, and then she watches the news for hours. With all the lights on.

ANGAD. Do you think she's doing okay?

MALICKA. She loves it, she loves being the martyr. And she is compelled to engage in this intense... analysis of geopolitics with all the lights on at nine p.m. She can't help herself.

SANGEETA. Sounds like she needs to get laid.

MALICKA. I find it stressful just being around someone who is so… (*Hand gesture, 'up to here'.*) I might have to check myself into a hotel.

ANGAD. Don't do that. Come stay with us.

SANGEETA catches ANGAD's eye and widens her eyes: 'NO!'

I think she's exhausted. Now that I look back, Dad hasn't been right since Christmas and she's been doing a lot of the heavy lifting.

MALICKA. I spoke to Dad every week so yes I am aware of how sick and abandoned he was this last year.

SANGEETA. I don't think / it's fair to say he was abandoned –

ANGAD touches SANGEETA's arm, restraining her.

ANGAD. So who wants pizza?

MALICKA. Pizza?

The doorbell rings.

SANGEETA. Get it from Da Mario.

ANGAD. Two should be enough. What do you think?

SANGEETA. Get four, Angad –

She takes ANGAD's phone.

ANGAD. People don't want to stuff themselves and feel uncomfortable.

SANGEETA. You can't impose your eating disorder on everyone.

MALICKA. Don't forget I'm plant-based.

SANGEETA. Yup.

GYAN enters with ANGAD, also wearing glasses. She gives SANGEETA a warm hug.

GYAN. Hello, my darling. How are you feeling, is my brother taking care of you?

SANGEETA. He is.

ANGAD. Mal said you couldn't get the day off?

GYAN walks to the fridge, takes a big sigh and starts rifling through the contents.

GYAN. It's non-stop right now. Yesterday was the national changeover day so all my juniors have no clue about the IT and the system… One of them spent an hour with one patient and didn't document a word.

(*Sniffing a box.*) What's this?

SANGEETA. Carbonara. Check if it's still alright.

GYAN takes a fork from the dishwasher, wipes it on her shirt and starts eating the carbonara. She paces as she eats directly from the box.

GYAN. Then she waited till seven to run all of her plans past me. I don't know what they do in their hospital block but when they arrive they are just clueless.

SANGEETA. Angad, heat that up for her.

ANGAD goes to heat up the pasta.

GYAN. And the locums just clock off: 'I did my eight hours, this is what I had time for, if you want me to look at any blood tests after six that will be two hundred pounds an hour, thank you very much.'

ANGAD. There's pizza coming.

GYAN. Nobody wants to take ownership. Or responsibility.

MALICKA. It sounds like you're the only doctor in the surgery who actually cares! Maybe even the whole world.

MALICKA makes a backhand gesture that GYAN is insane to SANGEETA. SANGEETA ignores it, and resumes hanging up the laundry.

Where's your restroom please?

ANGAD. On the right, where you came in.

MALICKA leaves. GYAN receives the heated carbonara.

GYAN. I had to write a letter to a cardiologist today: 'No I will not follow up the results of this colonoscopy, the GMC is very clear that the doctor who requests a test must follow it up and I am not your houseman.' And I signed it off, 'Consultant in general practice.'

Anyway. (Deep sigh.) How are you both?

GYAN finally seems to notice where she is. She wipes food off her face.

Angad, go hang up the laundry. Sangeeta, you just relax.

ANGAD goes over to the clothes horse and takes over hanging the laundry. GYAN adds chilli sauce to her food.

SANGEETA. Why didn't you say something to her?

ANGAD. Who?

SANGEETA. When she tried to make out like we neglected your dad and she was the only one who did anything for him?

ANGAD. That's Malicka feeling guilty she wasn't here.

SANGEETA. No. She doesn't even realise that she should feel guilty because she says retarded stuff like that and you let her get away with it.

MALICKA returns from the toilet, rubbing hand cream up to her elbows. She sees ANGAD.

MALICKA. Wow, Angad doing the laundry, that feels good to see. Do you remember how pissed Dad got when we tried to make you do it?

ANGAD. He was such a character.

MALICKA. You've been in politics too long, you've started believing your own spin. Was that Ralph Hughes at the gurdwara?

ANGAD. Party Whip, not bad. Quite a few of the Shadow Cabinet came along too.

ACT ONE, SCENE THREE   39

MALICKA. I can't believe that man had the cheek to come to your father's funeral.

MALICKA *spots* GYAN*'s medical bag by the door as she enters.*

Why did you bring your doctor's bag into the house?

GYAN. Some of my colleagues have had their car broken into.

MALICKA *looks at* SANGEETA *significantly.* SANGEETA *pours herself another glass of wine.*

ANGAD. I think my speech went alright.

GYAN. It was really good, Splint.

ANGAD. Do you think I sounded like a potential leader?

GYAN. Laura Kuenssberg just called you a rising star.

ANGAD. What? When?

GYAN. On the radio, on my way here.

ANGAD. On the *Westminster Hour*?

He starts searching for the response himself on his phone.

MALICKA. Has he ever apologised for the way he treated you?

ANGAD. Who?

MALICKA. The way Ralph Hughes tormented you at that school.

ANGAD. It wasn't like that, we're mates.

MALICKA. 'How come you're so Indian but you're so shit at maths.' That is not something a mate says.

SANGEETA *bursts out laughing.*

SANGEETA. I'm sorry that is *so funny.*

MALICKA. He owes you an apology.

SANGEETA. To be fair, Angad, your maths is appalling, genuinely the whitest thing about you. Brown skin but shit at maths – (*She bends with laughter.*) that is amazing.

ANGAD. See, it's funny.

MALICKA. You were the only new boy coming from a state school and instead of welcoming you, he went out of his way to make you feel small and different and like you shouldn't be there.

ANGAD. Don't try to make it into a big deal.

MALICKA. He was racist and he bullied you. I walked in on you rubbing talc into your skin / before you –

ANGAD. Oh come on! / Thirty years ago…

MALICKA. …before you went to his house. Do you think all kids do that?

ANGAD. …How do you remember this stuff?

MALICKA. Gyan, can you back me up?

GYAN puts down the carbonara. With massive effort she goes back into the murky memory of childhood.

GYAN. I do remember you asking me to tell him we lived in Ealing when I collected you from his house.

MALICKA. There you go.

ANGAD. So what!

MALICKA. People aren't supposed to be afraid to tell their 'mates' they live in Southall.

SANGEETA. You pretended you lived in *Ealing*, jaan, that is so sweet. Never heard of the Royal Borough of Kensington and Chelsea?

MALICKA. Why can't you just admit it?

ANGAD. Admit what!

MALICKA. Are you still scared of him?

ANGAD. I am not scared of him. Sometimes things aren't a big deal, sometimes you're not traumatised and you don't think about it again / and when you do it's funny.

MALICKA. Traumatised, exactly.

ANGAD. Ralph's been a really good friend to me, and an ally in my campaign.

MALICKA. He is a bully.

GYAN. Malicka, can you drop this?

MALICKA. Fine. Fine.

GYAN looks at her phone and sighs.

GYAN. Shall we open it up then.

ANGAD. I thought we could eat first and then...

GYAN. I need to get going by ten.

MALICKA. You just arrived. Thirty minutes late.

GYAN. I'm on the early bird tomorrow which means I have to be out the house at six. That means waking up at five.

MALICKA. I think you can take one day off.

GYAN. I'm too tired to explain how much I have to do tomorrow.

MALICKA. Why do you do this to yourself?

GYAN. I'm single-handedly raising two boys, paying their fees which are extortionate by the way, caring for Dad, whilst I am the named responsible physician for five thousand patients and unlike you I am doing it alone.

MALICKA. You can take a day off.

ANGAD. The driver is on his way to collect our pizza!

GYAN. If I take a day off it doesn't stop, do you realise that?

MALICKA. I'm worried about you.

GYAN. I'm still catching up the work I missed yesterday.

SANGEETA stands up abruptly.

SANGEETA. I think I'm going to hit the hay.

GYAN. No! This is nothing, we aren't fighting.

SANGEETA. I didn't sleep well last night.

42   THE ESTATE

ANGAD *and* SANGEETA *kiss.*

ANGAD. Don't forget your vitamin.

SANGEETA. There's ice cream in the freezer if you want later.

GYAN. Goodnight, gorgeous. Will you let me know about lunch?

SANGEETA *pads out and goes upstairs.*

(*To* MALICKA.) Did you have to do that today?

MALICKA. What?

GYAN. All your Ralph Hughes shit-stirring. What is the point of that? (*Nodding after* SANGEETA.) Is she okay?

ANGAD. Her back's been playing up.

MALICKA *picks up family photos on a sideboard.*

MALICKA. She should read *The Body Keeps the Score.*

God I'm starving. It's something about crematoriums.

GYAN. I remember I had two Big Macs, one after the other, after Mum's funeral.

MALICKA. Who's this?

ANGAD. That's Sangeeta's grandparents.

GYAN. Should we open it up then?

GYAN *rinses her fork, accidentally spraying water on herself and dabbing herself clean.* MALICKA *puts on her reading glasses and pauses, struck by the image of the three of them.*

MALICKA. He would have hated this.

ANGAD. What?

She gestures to their glasses. ANGAD *shakes his head.*

MALICKA. He wouldn't let all three of us wear our glasses at the same time.

ANGAD. Really?

ACT ONE, SCENE THREE 43

MALICKA (*Indian accent*). 'People will say your genes are weak'? We had to take it in turns going blind, just for his vanity.

(*To* ANGAD.) Like he didn't want you becoming 'dependent' on your inhaler.

MALICKA *looks to her siblings for validation. She gets none.* GYAN *starts to open the will.*

GYAN. You're talking about 1998. I don't think Dad was like that by the end.

MALICKA. Wow. Amazing. I've spent my whole life trying to forget what he said / and you've just...

GYAN. But Dad had such a soft spot for you.

MALICKA. No, I'm happy for you. I wish I could unhear it too.

GYAN. He let you get away with murder!

MALICKA. Only because I learnt what he wanted from me. He saw me as an extension of himself, that's the only way I was safe. My therapist thinks he was a narcissist.

GYAN. That's a medical term, he should be very careful / diagnosing –

ANGAD *puts a hand on* GYAN, *quietening her.*

MALICKA. My therapist is a woman.

ANGAD. Let Mal diagnose Dad if it helps her.

MALICKA. You should talk about it. All this repression is going to end up as chronic pain.

GYAN *sits down at the table with* MALICKA *and* ANGAD. *They open the envelope and start to read the pages. A stunned silence.*

GYAN *takes an enormous sigh.* MALICKA *angrily flicks through the pages, looking for some mention of her name but she's not in there. Nor is* GYAN.

MALICKA *stands, her chair scraping the floor, and starts to pace.*

Did you know he was going to do this?

ANGAD. No.

MALICKA. Bullshit.

ANGAD. I didn't know.

MALICKA *leaves the room.* GYAN *looks like she's been punched.*

GYAN. I didn't think he'd make it equal. But I didn't think he'd do this.

MALICKA *returns, holding a bottle of Chivas Regal.*

MALICKA. You think he changed? Let me introduce you to our dad, still shitting on us from beyond the grave and it's not 1998 by the way.

MALICKA *pours herself a generous portion of Chivas.*

No mention of either of his daughters in his last will and testament. Nice one, Dad. And nice one leaving us to find out like this.

(*To* GYAN.) Do you want one?

GYAN *shakes her head.*

GYAN. Angad?

MALICKA *pushes the bottle towards* ANGAD.

MALICKA. Yeah apologies if I don't feel like serving the heir apparent anything on a plate right now.

I mean this is so fucked up, this backwards, patriarchal – it's practically Tudor, all this obsession with a son. For what?

ANGAD. Why are you looking at me?

MALICKA. To take over his shitty property portfolio, it's actually gross, you know these are modern-day slums bought through a lifetime of tax evasion – some fucking legacy, Dad.

GYAN. Okay we all heard you –

MALICKA. I can't believe he's fucking done this, I cannot believe he has done this / after everything he put me through.

GYAN. Okay. Okay. Malicka, please. Malicka, that's *enough*.

We just left his funeral. Our dad just died. Can we please just focus on all the good stuff he did?

MALICKA *drains her Chivas.*

MALICKA. I don't know why he was so precious about this stuff, it's absolutely vile.

Beat.

ANGAD. How are your boys?

GYAN. They're heartbroken. Raja wanted to do his end-of-year art project on him.

ANGAD. That's so sweet – (*Sniffs.*) Will you share it on the group?

GYAN. He's really talented, he does these...

She shows ANGAD *her phone.*

It's been really good for his confidence after his GCSEs. Look at this.

ANGAD *looks at the picture, starts to fiddle his nose.*

ANGAD. Amazing, Gyan. This is so good.

MALICKA. Can you just blow your nose?

ANGAD. What?

She slams a box of tissues in front of him.

I'm sorry, am I missing something?

MALICKA (*imitates a snotty voice*). 'I'm sorry am I missing something?' / It's disgusting. Blow it.

ANGAD. Why are you so angry at me? What have I done?

GYAN. Malicka. It's not fair to punish Angad for something Dad did. He's said it's wrong.

ANGAD. Thank you.

GYAN. He's not our dad.

ANGAD. Exactly.

GYAN. He always said he'll share it.

ANGAD. Mmm.

MALICKA. Angad?

ANGAD. Of course I will. I think that's the right thing to do.

GYAN. We need to stick together right now, more than ever. No one else will ever understand what Dad was like. We need to be there for each other.

ANGAD. Thank you, Gyan.

MALICKA. Fine. I'll call Dad's lawyer tomorrow.

ANGAD. Okay.

MALICKA. I'll tell him you want to make it equal. I'm flying out on Wednesday, can we do Monday?

GYAN. Mondays are hard for me.

MALICKA. Tuesday?

GYAN. Fine by me.

ANGAD. Sounds good.

Beat. GYAN *starts eating.* MALICKA *opens one of the packets of crisps* SANGEETA *laid out earlier.*

Just to clarify. I never said I would make it equal.

MALICKA. Excuse me?

ANGAD. I want to be clear.

MALICKA. You just said it's the right thing.

ANGAD *makes to speak but no words come out.*

WHAT?!

ANGAD. I don't think Dad should have written you out.

MALICKA. Well done.

GYAN. But what?

ANGAD. And I would like to make a gesture –

MALICKA. What does that mean?

ANGAD. ... but I need to think about this.

MALICKA. Spit it out.

ANGAD. I am about to become a father. I have responsibilities and pressures on me that you especially do not face. And I think it is reasonable that I can take time to reflect before you just demand that I sign over two-thirds of my inheritance.

GYAN. Your inheritance?

ANGAD. Yes, my inheritance. It's literally mine, I'm being asked to give it away. What's the problem?

MALICKA. The inheritance that's yours because of Dad's sexism.

ANGAD. That is an opinion, it's not a fact.

MALICKA. This is so / predictable.

GYAN. But I remember you telling me fifteen years ago, you wish you could split it with me there and then.

ANGAD. I didn't say 'equal'.

GYAN. 'Why should I get more? It just doesn't make sense.'

MALICKA. Because now he's / benefitting.

GYAN. No, sorry, Malicka – I want to hear this.

Why the change of heart?

ANGAD. Well, maybe fifteen years ago I would have but I'm in a very different position now.

MALICKA. Yeah / because when it's in your –

GYAN. What's different?

ANGAD. Well firstly, I went into politics. I left my law career…

MALICKA. What law career?

ANGAD. …and that was a big financial sacrifice I made. To go into public service. To try to make things better for everyone.

MALICKA *laughs loudly.*

MALICKA. A law degree is not a law career.

ANGAD. And Dad wanted to support me in that! Dad wanted to support the sacrifices I've made for this family.

GYAN. Do you think you sacrificed more than me?

ANGAD. Don't give me that.

GYAN. Give you what?

ANGAD. Be honest with yourself. I had pressures on me that you never had.

GYAN. Do you think you did more for Dad than I did?

ANGAD. I do. But I will acknowledge one thing. At least you were here.

MALICKA *makes a squeal of frustrated rage. She starts to splash* ANGAD *with water from her glass.*

MALICKA. You little rat.

GYAN. Alright. Stop that. Guys.

ANGAD *steps away. He pulls out a dining chair to keep* MALICKA *away from him; she tries to get around it.*

MALICKA. You slimy little weasel.

GYAN. Can you try to understand how much this hurts?

We are trying to come to terms with a lifetime of being told we weren't good enough, no matter what we did for Dad.

ANGAD. I agree, that's wrong.

GYAN. Can you imagine how it feels?

MALICKA. Yeah, use your fucking imagination / and try to see what we went through.

ANGAD. No. You can't speak to me like that. At least Gyan was here, at least she was trying. Malicka, where have you been the last decade?

MALICKA. If he'd had three sons do you think this would have been equal?

ANGAD. That's a mad question! If he'd had three sons everything would have been different. He would have stopped at one, given it all to him!

GYAN. Answer the question, Angad, what would Dad have done for three sons?

ANGAD. I'm not a bloody witch, how do I know?

MALICKA. Because you know our dad, fucking answer the question –

ANGAD. I'm not speaking to you if you speak to me like that –

GYAN. *Pleaaase*. What would he have done for three sons?

ANGAD. Fine. He would have made it equal.

MALICKA. No matter what we did, or where we lived, so you don't have a leg to stand on, you fucking hypocrite.

GYAN. If you don't change the will, you're saying what Dad did to us was okay.

ANGAD. What did he do to you?

MALICKA. We had to cook for you, clean up after you. We had to pray that you would be a boy, no more girls, do you see how fucked up that is?

GYAN. Can you see, it's not about money, Angad.

ANGAD. Question: if it's not about money, how come money can fix it?

MALICKA. This isn't very smart of you. Aren't you running for election?

ANGAD. I've done nothing wrong.

MALICKA. Well, I'm sure it could be pretty embarrassing if people find out what a misogynist you are.

ANGAD. A misogynist?! I do the laundry, I go down on my wife.

MALICKA. Well, it's time to put your money where your mouth is!

ANGAD. Don't try to make out that I'm / some kind of –

MALICKA. A primitive, backwards misogynist.

ANGAD. 'Primitive'!

MALICKA. You're not 'Mr Modern', 'Mr Laundry', are you?

ANGAD. Most men would do a lot less.

MALICKA. This is a lot more pindoo than living in Southall.

ANGAD laughs, seeing her misstep and the point he has scored.

ANGAD. You are so vicious! Dad's primitive? Barbaric? Our wokest little warrior is the first one to get racist when it suits her.

MALICKA. Argh!!

MALICKA picks up a cushion and throws it at him.

ANGAD. / Hey!

MALICKA. Do you have any idea how embarrassing all this is? I can't even tell my husband / what you lot are actually like –

ANGAD. Why do you think you're such victims! Malicka, you haven't worked for a decade, you cannot pretend you need money now, / *I don't believe you.*

MALICKA. That is none of your business.

ANGAD. And you – (*To* GYAN.) You just told us that your locums earn two hundred pounds an hour.

GYAN. I have never done a day of private work / in my career –

ANGAD. What's stopping you?! You want money, it's there for you to take –

GYAN. That's / not me –

ANGAD. First time you two decide to show any ambition it's at your brother's house / for some cash your dad didn't want you to have –

MALIKCA (*imitating* ANGAD *from earlier*). 'It's wrong. I agree. I'm sorry, guys, I didn't know.' Pathetic.

ANGAD. I said I would make a gesture!

MALICKA. Fuck your gesture, we should all get a third.

ANGAD. Says who!

MALICKA. You just said it's what he would have done for three sons.

Beat.

GYAN. Please, please, *please* we need to, we all need to stop. This has been a horrible, horrible, horrible day and this is getting so ugly you need to stop, please just stop.

ANGAD. She's right. You're right. We should put a pin in this conversation and pick it up when we're ready to speak calmly.

GYAN. We're hungry, we're tired, and I've got a horrible headache and this day has been bad enough already. So please, please can we stop.

Beat.

ANGAD. You okay?

MALICKA. I've got some Tylenol in my bag, do you want one?

GYAN *nods*. ANGAD *goes to get a glass of water as* MALICKA *gets the tablets*.

Here, take the night one.

GYAN. Thank you.

ANGAD. Here you go, Gee.

GYAN. Thanks.

ANGAD. The pizza will be here soon if you want to take one with you.

MALICKA looks at the time.

MALICKA. Isn't it funny how you can't organise dinner on time.

GYAN. Just leave it.

MALICKA. I'm just saying that it's funny.

The pakoras got to the gurdwara on time – (*Points to* GYAN.) The flowers got to the crematorium – (*Pointing to herself.*) But when it's time for dinner at Angad's… (*A gesture to suggest he's incompetent.*)

ANGAD. Oh let me guess, it's all because Dad was sexist.

MALICKA. Do you think we came out the womb knowing how to do this?

GYAN. *Please.*

ANGAD. Alright. Sorry. And for the record, I told him he should make it equal.

Beat. A shriek sounds out from upstairs. ANGAD looks up the stairs but his sisters stare at him.

MALICKA. What?

ANGAD. That's right.

GYAN. So you knew?

Beat.

ANGAD. I was aware there was a chance.

MALICKA. You are such a fucking slippery politician! We can't believe a word you say.

ANGAD. Hang on let's just calm down, I didn't trick him.

ACT ONE, SCENE THREE 53

GYAN. You didn't think to mention this to me?

ANGAD. This was his choice, not mine, that's all I'm saying.

SANGEETA *runs down the stairs in her pyjamas.*

I'm the good guy.

SANGEETA. *Did you eat their cum?* –

She bends over, retching.

ANGAD. What's wrong?

MALICKA. Can you stay out of this?

GYAN. / I can't do this.

GYAN *goes to the freezer and starts binging ice cream on autopilot.*

SANGEETA. Are you going to let her speak to me like that?

ANGAD. Don't speak to my wife like that.

SANGEETA. I can't believe this is happening.

ANGAD. What's the matter, Sangeeta?

SANGEETA. Did you do it?

MALICKA. We're actually in the middle of something right now.

SANGEETA. Tell me you didn't do it?

ANGAD. *Do what?*

SANGEETA. *Swallow a pile of cum.*

ANGAD. What are you talking about?

SANGEETA. Soggy biscuit?!

SANGEETA *shows* ANGAD *the social media newsreel on her phone. Horror dawns on* ANGAD's *face as he listens.*

NEWS (*voice-over*).... source who was at school with both Mr Singh and Mr Hughes and described it as a competitive masturbation game / which boys would play over cocoa...

ANGAD. Rollo? No… / No…

SANGEETA. Is this true?

MALICKA. We're actually in the middle of something.

SANGEETA (*still retching*). I think I'm going to be sick.

ANGAD *starts hyperventilating.*

ANGAD. Oh my God. / Oh my God –

SANGEETA. What were you thinking?

ANGAD. I can't breathe –

SANGEETA. Why did you do it?

ANGAD. I was fifteen years old –

SANGEETA. *That's your answer?*

ANGAD. It was banter.

SANGEETA. Do you think this is what fifteen-year-olds do?

ANGAD. It was banter, Sangeeta.

SANGEETA. It's not funny, / it is not funny.

ANGAD. Do you have any idea what it was like being the one Indian in that school? The things I had to do / to get –

SANGEETA. Don't you dare make this about yourself.

GYAN (*with a mouthful of ice cream*). Sangeeta, what's going on.

SANGEETA. Your brother sat in a room of future leaders of this country and they all touched themselves together in a circle until they came on a biscuit. And because your brother was the last one to cum, he *ate that biscuit.*

A stunned silence. MALICKA *laughs with utter glee.*

GYAN. No. You didn't.

MALICKA. Oh this is too good.

GYAN. Angad, no?

ACT ONE, SCENE THREE

MALICKA. It's a metaphor for your entire career.

GYAN. Why did you do that?

ANGAD. I had no choice.

SANGEETA. There seems like a pretty obvious choice.

GYAN. Angad, why would you do that?

ANGAD roars. The women have never seen him like this before.

ANGAD. IT. WAS. BANTER.

Getting naked and being towel-whipped and putting your arse in Rollo's face if he took the top bunk, you had to. You had to get blacked out if the King of Bus said so, on the floor you had to crawl through the gauntlet, everyone punching and kicking and their balls are in your face. You had to do it. *If you didn't, it was GAY.* Do you understand? It was gay if you *didn't* do it, that's what everyone / said, so I had to.

SANGEETA. It's okay, it's okay. I understand.

ANGAD. MY FATHER SENT ME THERE IN A FUCKING TURBAN.

SANGEETA. I understand, / it's okay –

ANGAD. He wouldn't let me shave and I had fucking bumfluff all over my face it was disgusting I was disgusting do you understand? I had / to sing hymns louder than everyone else and whip towels and be the king of banter.

SANGEETA. It's okay, love.

ANGAD. Every time he came down he made it worse – he used to make a big fucking show of slipping me a fiver in front of everyone like it was a huge deal meanwhile everyone else's parents are there being so tasteful and discreet about fifties and my dad is *loooording* his fucking fiver over me –

SANGEETA. I know, it's okay,

ANGAD. He was so tacky and humiliating / in the way that only an Indian man can be.

SANGEETA. Just take this.

SANGEETA brings ANGAD's inhaler to him. ANGAD puffs from it, like a pacifier.

ANGAD. So I did what I had to do. / I had to.

SANGEETA. I know.

ANGAD. They crucified me.

SANGEETA. It's okay.

Pause.

GYAN. Are you okay?

ANGAD nods. Beat.

MALICKA. I wish Dad was around. Asthmatic, on your knees in front of your wife – fattened up on posh-boy semen. He would have written you out of this will right now.

GYAN (*looking at* ANGAD). Maybe this isn't the time…

MALICKA. He would have wanted the estate to go to someone he could actually be proud of.

She looks at herself and GYAN.

Some patriarch you turned out to be.

GYAN. She didn't mean that.

Beat.

ANGAD. I'll kill you.

MALICKA. You're going to kill me?

ANGAD. How dare you –

SANGEETA. I think perhaps we should put a pin in this conversation and pick it up / when we're ready to speak calmly.

MALICKA. I'm not leaving till he sorts out my father's / will –

ANGAD. Your father! Your father is a bastard! I hope he rots in hell for what he did to me.

MALICKA. What he did to you?

ANGAD. HOW DARE YOU COME HERE –

MALICKA. At least you got compensated for it –

ANGAD. HOW DARE YOU COME TO MY SANCTUARY –

SANGEETA. He's been feeling very sensitive –

MALICKA. He's feeling sensitive?

SANGEETA. Your father was very critical / of him –

MALICKA. I'm the one receiving death threats –

ANGAD. I will murder you.

GYAN. Okay, guys, everyone needs to calm down.

ANGAD. GET OUT.

MALICKA. I'm not going anywhere.

GYAN. Shhh / shhhhhhh –

ANGAD. GET OUT OF MY HOUSE –

GYAN. Let's all stay calm.

MALICKA. Make me then! Make me.

ANGAD. LEAVE.

GYAN claps her hands to claim attention.

GYAN. Alright, everybody, that's enough. That is enough! We are leaving!

GYAN picks up MALICKA*'s coat and holds it out for* MALICKA, *but she doesn't take it.* GYAN *starts to lead* MALICKA *out.*

(*To* ANGAD.) You know what's right and what's wrong. I know you'll fix the will.

ANGAD. Is the will broken?

MALICKA turns back into the room, as GYAN continues to try and pull her out.

MALICKA. You know, death by testicular cancer would be too good for you.

The doorbell rings as ANGAD *screams at* MALICKA.

ANGAD. It's always about my testicles with you, YOU'RE OBSESSED, YOU SHOULD TALK TO YOUR THERAPIST ABOUT THAT.

MALICKA (*as* GYAN *finally pulls her out of the room*). You're a little shit, you always have been.

SANGEETA *goes to open the door, following behind the exiting sisters.*

ANGAD *stands frozen, his hand to his face in contemplation.*

SANGEETA (*offstage*). Thank you. That's great. Thanks.

PIZZA MAN (*offstage*). Sorry, I got a bit lost.

SANGEETA (*offstage*). Not to worry.

PIZZA MAN (*offstage*). I thought this was Carlton Road.

SANGEETA (*offstage*). Yeah, a lot of people make that mistake. Carlton Road's up / that way –

PIZZA MAN (*offstage*). Yeah behind the roundabout. Cheers, have a good evening.

SANGEETA (*offstage*). You too. Thanks.

SANGEETA *returns carrying four boxes of pizza, and stares at* ANGAD.

ANGAD. Did I lose my cool?

End of Act One.

ACT TWO

Scene One

Angad's office – ISAAC *and* PETRA *sit at their desks, typing.*

ISAAC. Man, I didn't realise Angad was so white.

PETRA. He's not.

ISAAC. Eating your friend's cum? In a game?

That is some extremely white juju.

Beat. ISAAC *clicks on his computer. He's looking at the news, not working.*

Do you ever feel kinda jealous of Greta? Like I was worried about the climate when I was a kid too but my parents just told me to get on with it. They never supported me like that. Greta's parents are in PR you know.

No wonder she's been nominated for two Nobels.

PETRA. Yeah your parents got that one really wrong.

Scrolling through her phone.

ISAAC. Plus she's winter-born. I'm August.

PETRA. Angad's being flayed in the Spad WhatsApp group... It's degrading.

Do you think I should be working for Dobson?

ISAAC. What? Why the hell would you want to work for that guy?

PETRA. I know he's got the – (*Gesture of tickling.*) but people seem to think this is worse.

ISAAC. Petra, no. This is the team to be on.

Did you ever read Angad's paper on salaried GPs, or central funding for trees? Let me find it for you. You can't abandon him over some schoolboy weird stuff.

He's creative, he's got vision, don't forget that.

PETRA. I suppose if I was going to jump ship, Wednesday would have been the time do it – that wonderful moment when he was ahead in the polls. And I suppose when we were ahead in the polls it didn't make sense anyway…

ISAAC. I sent that to you now.

PETRA. Our careers are flies to the wanton god of public opinion.

ISAAC. So you're on our team now?

PETRA. Hundred per cent.

ISAAC. Fucking hell.

Pause. They pretend to work. PETRA *grimaces at a vicious meme of* ANGAD.

PETRA. I can't believe he thought this wouldn't come out.

ISAAC. I think you need to connect to that thing that gets you through difficult times. Remember why you're here.

He gestures to his heart.

PETRA. If you're going to talk about religion I'd like a chaperone.

ISAAC. What made you go into politics?

Fuck, I gotta take my creatine…

He starts to rummage through his rucksack.

PETRA. You think I should've done law?

ISAAC *is surprised to find an apple in his bag. He doesn't take his creatine. He starts eating the apple.*

ISAAC. It's not a trick question.

It's not even a hard question.

No one sleepwalks into the palace of Westminster, so tell me: why are you here?

Why are you suddenly so shy?

PETRA. I'm not shy.

ISAAC. Why can't you tell me?

You want me to tell you why I'm here?

PETRA. *No*. Please no! Fine. Why I did politics?

I suppose I picked politics because Dr Hackett taught it.

ISAAC *remembers his creatine and now goes to take it.*

He had a PhD from Yale and this soft East Coast accent. And his lectures on Whig England were superb, I can remember every word.

ISAAC *googles Dr Hackett while* PETRA *speaks*.

It was this razor-sharp analysis but then he'd like slide in these references to Nietzsche and Francis Ford Coppola movies so yes, I thought about him all the time.

ISAAC. This guy?

PETRA. He doesn't photograph well.

ISAAC. So the guy inspired you?

PETRA. It was an all-girls' school, Isaac. He inspired all of us.

ISAAC. He made you believe that politics mattered?

PETRA. No, I wouldn't say that. It was somewhere between wanting to be like him and wanting him to think I was pretty, not just pretty, I guess special and clever and so full of potential that he'd risk his career by making a move on me.

ISAAC. He got his PhD in 1998, fucking hell.

PETRA. He never did groom me in the end, but I did get a first in PPE.

ISAAC. This is mad. You've made it here, to the seat of power, whispering into the ears that write the laws and when I ask you why you wanna be here, that's all you got?

Fucking hell. You should leave Zone Two and go see how people live in this country. Come and see how people live where I'm from.

Did you tell Angad about the Yale prof in your interview?

PETRA. Of course I did, Isaac.

I told him all about how my parents had a horrible divorce when I was ten so now I'm strangely drawn to men in their forties because you see Daddy was forty-five when he moved out and it's this confusing, heady desperation to both be like them and also be special to them, and it started with Dr Hackett but maybe now it could transfer to Angad because it makes me work very, very hard for reasons that aren't even clear to me but make me very good at my job.

I said all this to Angad and it rang with such truth that he hired me on the spot. Because in politics that's what everyone's really looking for, right? Someone who tells the truth when they're asked a penetrating question.

ISAAC. I told Angad he had shown me how / politicians can –

PETRA. And no thank you, I don't want to know what got you here.

I actually think it's private.

ANGAD *enters. He storms though the office and goes straight to his desk.* ISAAC *stands out of his chair.*

ISAAC. Did you guys see that sketch I sent you / about the party conference –

ANGAD. Who's been touching my desk?

PETRA. I haven't.

ISAAC. I literally just sat down.

ANGAD *goes to make a coffee.*

I think the cleaning lady might have moved some stuff, she's new.

PETRA. I can have a word with her if you'd like?

Beat. ANGAD *starts picking up mugs, looking for a clean one.*

ANGAD. I think I must be the only member of the Commons who has to wash his own mug before he makes his own coffee in his own office. Whilst a cleaner comes in to fiddle his drawers but ignores a stack of dirty mugs stained with lipstick, all the while his team stands and watches him, it really is amazing.

PETRA *pulls a clean mug out of the cabinet.*

PETRA. Let me make that for you, Angad. Did you want a double or single?

ANGAD *lets* PETRA *take over and returns to his desk. He slams a drawer three times.*

Let's stick to single, shall we?

I want to start by saying that I for one didn't watch the Rollo interview. I didn't want to dignify it with another view.

ANGAD. You didn't watch it?

PETRA. I did not.

And I think we should remember, it's only the party members who get to vote next week.

PETRA *hands* ANGAD *a coffee.*

Half of them won't watch the clip, and the other half... I'd bet most of them played soggy biscuit themselves.

ANGAD *laughs to himself and starts pulling a* Metro *newspaper out of his briefcase.*

It's perfectly natural in a certain environment. Isn't that right, Isaac.

ISAAC. I've seen posh people kiss their dogs on the mouth with tongues.

PETRA. Precisely. We mustn't let a blip like this get us down. Anyone doing well is bound to attract some worms out the woodwork, and I hope you don't mind me saying that Rollo sounds like a real piece of shit.

ANGAD *spreads his newspaper on the desk.*

There's still everything to play for at the conference this weekend.

ANGAD. Well, there's my answer.

All morning I've been asking myself, 'What is my communication team doing?'

Because over the last two days, two news stories came out that were equally embarrassing for me and Dobson. That's how it seems to me, what do you think, Isaac?

ISAAC. Honestly I think his is worse in the current climate, / did you read that piece on...

ANGAD. Thank you, Isaac, I can see what you mean.

Arguably, his is more recent, it refers to his actions as an adult and yeah, I can see how arguably it says more about his suitability to lead the party. I think that's fair.

ISAAC. Yeah, his is definitely worse.

PETRA....

ANGAD (*cutting in before* PETRA *can speak*). And you, of course, Petra, can't comment because you didn't watch the video.

PETRA. Well, I am aware of the contents.

ANGAD. But when I read the morning papers I see that somehow, I am a laughing stock and Dobson is polling ahead of me with both the members and the public. Why?

PETRA. Well. Dobson's camp probably had their response prepared for years, it was a matter of time before this story / hit the –

ACT TWO, SCENE ONE 65

ANGAD. I thought I also employed a comms team to think about those things.

PETRA. You could have warned us this was lurking in the background. Before the tickle story went out and... mud started flying.

ANGAD. You didn't watch the video.

You didn't watch the video.

PETRA. I didn't want to fuel a story that is potentially embarrassing for us.

ANGAD. Why is this the first front-page headline of my career?

PETRA. That's not fair. Your visit to Regent's Park Mosque had a teaser on the front page / of *The i* –

ANGAD. Maybe I should ask Edward Dobson where he found his team, he's come off looking like a really cool guy. Dobson's a tickle lad and I'm just an asthmatic loser. Is that right?

ISAAC. It's not like that.

ANGAD. Why is this the story everyone's telling about me?

ISAAC. It's not the story we're telling.

ANGAD. Where's my family tragedy and my love for the nurses? And my dad coming here with five pounds in his pocket.

Where's my story? What have you been doing?

PETRA. I'm sorry, Angad.

ANGAD. I'm sorry what?

PETRA. It's not good enough.

ANGAD. I am supposed to have the brightest minds in the country behind me, and I've come off worse after the revelation of my own childhood sexual abuse! You cannot write this level of shitness.

'Didn't watch the video.'

PETRA. I'll do better.

ANGAD. Isaac, what are you doing?

ISAAC. I'm working on the carers' / policy document we discussed.

ANGAD. No! Stop that! I am running for the leadership and you need to work on this: my manifesto, my campaign, my story. Isn't that obvious?

ISAAC. Sure thing, that's right. I'll start that.

ANGAD. And how many tabs have you got open here... 'Greta Thunberg age'?

'Youngest Nobel laureate'.

'Octordle', what the fuck!

ISAAC. I'm sorry, boss.

ANGAD. I'm supposed to have a team! Not me on my own, against the bastards. You're supposed to be behind me!

ANGAD *starts to storm out.*

PETRA. Do you want me to / start drafting?

ANGAD. I want you to *be smart*.

ANGAD *leaves. The door slams.*

PETRA. I've never seen him like this before.

ISAAC. He's right. We should've been better.

ANGAD *returns with* RALPH, *who has picked him up in the corridor.*

RALPH *has his arm around* ANGAD, *urging him back into the office and making sure no one sees this.*

ISAAC *knocks Angad's offending* Metro *newspaper on the floor and* PETRA *kicks it under the table, out of sight.*

RALPH. I warned you that our leadership contests are brutal, Angad. Knives start flying and the whole party gets caught in the shit.

ACT TWO, SCENE ONE 67

I've told the committee to expect your withdrawal by the end of day.

ANGAD. Our response is in hand. Isn't it, Petra?

PETRA *nods. Studious and focused at her desk.*

RALPH. I don't know why you thought you could shoot your shot but you really fucked it.

I presume you've seen the memes?

ANGAD *nods.* RALPH *shows* ANGAD *his screen.*

ANGAD. Yup I saw that one.

RALPH. Very creative.

ANGAD. Petra, could you bring Ralph a coffee?

RALPH. I assured Edward you were behind him, and this party does not reward treachery.

You are looking at three years so deep in the backbenches, Rural Affairs will seem like a distant, impossible dream.

ANGAD. Are you seriously still suggesting that Edward Dobson is the man to lead the party?

RALPH. Do the right thing for the party now, and I'll see what I can do to save you from total obscurity.

Can I tell the committee you'll go quietly?

Beat. RALPH *squeezes* ANGAD*'s shoulder.*

This isn't you... You're not the batsman. I remember you sitting out from cricket, clutching that inhaler for dear life, keeping score in the pavilion.

PETRA *hands* RALPH *a coffee.*

ANGAD. You're thinking of Li Wei Ping.

RALPH. Am I?

ANGAD. Yes. I like cricket.

RALPH. Of course you do.

> Edward has that quality that's very hard to quantify but just so vital for leadership: our members trust him.
>
> I thought you understood that.

ISAAC. But to be fair, since then, new information came out about Dobson – (*Tickle gesture.*)

ANGAD. Thank you, Isaac. That is a smart observation.

> Petra, can you bring Ralph something to have with his coffee?

PETRA *leaves the room.*

RALPH. I've burnt through a decade of favours with the press to bury – (*Tickle gesture.*) because it's better than a contest where every pervert in the party gets caught in their dirty knickers.

ANGAD. What's Edward Dobson's vision for the party? Lie low and wait for the government to fuck up so badly that we start to look good in comparison?

RALPH. It's proved effective in the past.

> The government is falling, very slowly, onto their own sword. All we have to do is look faintly competent with normal, normal-to-edgy sexual appetites, and the next election is in the bag.

Ping. RALPH *gets an email and immediately starts responding.*

ISAAC. No! No, that's where you're wrong.

> We lost because we didn't have any vision! No one knows what Edward Dobson stands for, whereas Angad can offer the party and the country a clear story: we are the party of...

RALPH. Mmm.

ANGAD. Let's all wait for Ralph to finish.

RALPH. Mmm.

Beat. RALPH *realises* ANGAD *won't let* ISAAC *continue until he has* RALPH*'s attention. He finishes his email and puts his phone away.*

ANGAD. What you were saying, Isaac?

ISAAC. Angad can position us as the party of ordinary aspiration. That's how we win the next General. He'll bring in a crowd who never voted for us before, people who thought the party wasn't for them.

PETRA *re-enters with a plate of Hobnobs.*

PETRA. People like Isaac.

ISAAC *makes a face.* PETRA *mouths: What?!*

RALPH. You think middle England can relate to Angad after this?!

ANGAD *offers* RALPH *the Chocolate Hobnobs.*

No.

ANGAD. You're sure?

Because. Because the way I remember it. You always... loved... biscuits.

I remember you having such a sweet tooth.

You kept your sweet tooth after everyone else had really grown out of it, way after school. After your twenty-first.

Archie's. Stag.

ANGAD *pushes the biscuit towards* RALPH.

Beat.

If Dobson steps away now, I'm prepared to offer him a prominent position in my Shadow Cabinet.

I want to bring the party together in a broad church, with a clear vision and agenda to offer the British public.

A long pause.

RALPH. Who's managing your campaign?

ANGAD. Petra.

RALPH. I would recommend that you focus more on your national profile.

PETRA. We've been targeting the House and the members who actually / have a vote next week.

RALPH. The members are trying to read the public for a man who can get us through the General.

ISAAC. That's right. We need to let people hear what Angad has to say. Let them see how he's different.

Beat.

RALPH. I've been calling for Dobson's anointment since the resignation, you understand.

ANGAD. But you've never been afraid of controversy. (*Laughing.*) Do you remember the first New College bop?

RALPH *surveys* ANGAD *intently, trying to read him.*

RALPH. I can't say that I...

ANGAD. The theme was 'your worst nightmare' and you... (*Laughs.*) You came as... I really must find the photos. They're really funny.

RALPH. The photos.

ANGAD. I suppose it was a different time.

Pause.

RALPH. You've made some really strong points, strategically / and um...

ANGAD. Ideologically?

RALPH. Ideologically. And I'm starting to think that a contest is the best way to put a clear choice to our members.

ANGAD. I think it's the best for the party.

RALPH. Yup, yup.

I'll ensure no other candidates enter the contest and privately, when the moment's right, I think I may suggest to Teddy...

ANGAD. Teddy?

RALPH. I will put it to Edward, that he might step aside for a prominent position in your Shadow Cabinet.

RALPH *stands*.

ANGAD. If you think that's best for the party. I appreciate it.

ANGAD *walks him out*.

I wanted to thank you for coming to the gurdwara. I think it would have meant a lot to my dad to have you there.

RALPH. Good to give the old man a decent send-off.

National profile, did you hear that?

A gesture to suggest: 'Get to work.'

RALPH *lingers, by the door and out of earshot of* PETRA *and* ISAAC.

Your profile is going to ramp up substantially, Gads, are you sure you want this?

ANGAD. Look at me. I'm ready.

RALPH. It'll be a bloodbath. Whatever dirt you're hiding it will come out.

Unpaid parking tickets? Unacknowledged children in the Home Counties?

I know it doesn't seem like it, but you've been spared a lot of scrutiny.

ANGAD. I have no skeletons.

RALPH. If you tell me now, I can bury them and they will never be a problem.

If you don't tell me about them, they have a way of becoming front-page news at the worst possible moment, as you've seen.

ANGAD. My closets are clean, Ralph. I'm the change.

RALPH. Fine. Good. I'll prepare the ground.

Your speech at the conference is your chance to convince the members.

RALPH *leaves*. PETRA *prints a document*.

ISAAC. You wouldn't want Dobson to have a major position in your Shadow Cabinet, would you, boss?

ANGAD. Nah. He didn't get me to write it down.

PETRA. Here's my response strategy / to yesterday's soggy –

ANGAD. Yeah.

PETRA. Denial; deflection and defiance. It's not relevant, it's not true and you're not dignifying it with air time.

ANGAD. Good.

PETRA. And if the press needs something to bury it with… I found the clip Dobson was watching on the Commons Wi-Fi. It's gross.

ANGAD. Correct.

PETRA. We shift the narrative to talking about your campaign promises, your policies and yes, Isaac's right, your story. It's powerful and it shows your vision for the party.

ANGAD. Well done. This is what I want to see. Thank you, team.

ANGAD *stands to leave but pauses by the door.*

And do up a button, you're at work.

ANGAD *leaves*.

ISAAC. Are you okay?

PETRA. Yeah. Fine.

ISAAC. Was Angad blackmailing him?

PETRA. It was on the line.

ISAAC. But Angad's got to show that he's different. Otherwise, what's going to change when he wins?

PETRA. That's very touching but in the end, as my grandmother used to say, I think you'll find one man is quite like another.

Scene Two

Singh household. SANGEETA *looks for her phone as* ANGAD*'s face appears on the news.*

NEWS (*voice-over*).... for the party conference this weekend, where the final two contenders for the party leadership, Edward Dobson and Angad Singh, will no doubt be battling to canvas members' support ahead of next week's ballot.

SANGEETA *rewinds the news clip and records it on her phone.*

...delegates are heading to Essex for the party conference this weekend, where the final two contenders for the party's leadership, Edward Dobson and Angad Singh, will no doubt be battling to canvas members' support ahead of next week's ballot.

The doorbell rings. SANGEETA *pauses the screen on* ANGAD*'s face and goes to open the door.*

SANGEETA (*offstage*). Malicka. I thought you left yesterday?

MALICKA (*offstage*). I need to speak to Angad. Is he here?

SANGEETA. He's still at work, is everything okay?

MALICKA. I think he's blocked me.

SANGEETA. This isn't really a good time.

MALICKA. Can you let him know I'm here?

SANGEETA. This weekend is probably the biggest moment of his career.

I'm not trying to stop you. I'm asking you to wait till the conference is over. Wait till the contest is over.

MALICKA. I'm not asking for your permission. This is going to be really embarrassing for him

SANGEETA. What's going to be embarrassing for him?

The doorbell rings. SANGEETA *goes to open the door,* MALICKA *trails after her.*

MALICKA. What he's doing with the will. (*She gestures to the television.*)

It was his choice to become a showman and plaster his face on every television in the country, so I'm sorry but now the press and the public will care about what he's doing to us. He needs to wake up and do the right thing before it costs him the leadership.

GYAN *enters.*

SANGEETA. The press?!

MALICKA. We said eight. I waited in the car for twenty minutes. / I need the loo.

GYAN. I got stuck at work. I'm sorry!

MALICKA *exits to the toilet.*

Hi, darling, how are you?

SANGEETA. Malicka's talking about going to the press.

GYAN. I know.

SANGEETA. Has she forgotten that Angad's running for leadership right now and it is crucial that she shows up for him!

GYAN. That's why I'm here. They need to talk.

SANGEETA. It's not normal for her to spend her time replaying all the ways in which she was short-changed by your parents, and lay it at Angad's feet. She can't punish him for your dad and your culture.

GYAN. It's complicated, Sangeeta, / you know that.

SANGEETA. I know she pays a therapist three hundred dollars an hour to listen to her version of the past but just because she says it again and again, that doesn't make it true.

GYAN. It's hard for her to accept the way / things were in our house.

SANGEETA. This is not the way to resolve anything. You know once, *once*, my brother tried to complain about how much my wedding cost our mum and dad and I said 'Cool, no worries, why don't we sit down and calculate how much it cost for you to retake your A levels three times and the next time you want me to buy your kid a present or go to some effort for you and your family it's going to be a big no from me. And how do you think our relationship will fare if we start making calculations like that?'

MALICKA *returns from the toilet.*

GYAN (*to* SANGEETA). Maybe you could speak to him? Help him to see where we're coming from.

SANGEETA. No.

MALICKA. Why not?

SANGEETA. Because it's nothing to do with me.

GYAN. Angad always said he'd share it. He doesn't believe in this crap. He's too upset to think straight and he doesn't even realise it. Talk to him.

SANGEETA *shakes her head.*

MALICKA. Sangeeta, is everything okay?

SANGEETA. Everything is fine.

MALICKA. Why won't you say what you think?

SANGEETA. Because you need to sort this between yourselves.

MALICKA. What are you scared of?

SANGEETA. I'm not scared.

MALICKA. Come on, no one's this inert.

SANGEETA. I actually think your dad is allowed to give his money to whoever he wants! Man, woman, child, dog.

MALICKA. Dog?

SANGEETA. It's not your right, it's his choice.

MALICKA. *Dog?*

SANGEETA. Right and wrong doesn't come into it.

MALICKA. No. No. You don't believe that.

SANGEETA. And now is not the time to have this conversation, six days before the vote, when the whole country is watching your brother.

MALICKA. Then he should do the right thing! It doesn't mean I have to keep quiet.

SANGEETA. The right thing is for you to restrain yourself and get behind him.

GYAN puts out a hand to stop MALICKA *from responding.*

GYAN. We are behind him, you know that. He's our little brother and we are very happy he's doing so well.

MALICKA (*to* SANGEETA). You are so trapped.

SANGEETA. No, I'm not.

MALICKA. You're trapped and you don't even know it.

SANGEETA goes to get a can of Coke. She takes two painkillers.

I was the same, I thought I was Dad's special one, the son he never had, then bam, this fucking will, and I'm back in the servants' quarters with the other women, and guess what, my brother wants me there too.

GYAN. Sangeeta, can I have one?

SANGEETA. Go for it.

GYAN *takes a Coke out of the fridge.*

MALICKA. Meanwhile you're telling me Angad's career is the most important thing in the family. Can't you see how that's a trap?

SANGEETA. / Stop saying I'm trapped.

GYAN. Malicka!

SANGEETA. You barely saw your dad for the last decade, / I don't know why you think he owes you so much.

MALICKA. That's not fair, you know this is about the principle that we are worth / the same as Angad.

SANGEETA. There are lots of feminist principles that you are very happy to ignore. You've spent your life spending money that men have worked for so I don't know why you think / you've had it so hard.

MALICKA. THIS IS A MATTER OF LIFE AND DEATH, CAN YOU SEE THAT?

There are billboards in Punjab that say 'It's better to pay one lakh today to abort your daughters and save ten lakhs for when you have to pay for her dowry.'

SANGEETA. Please, don't conflate what you're doing with something important. I think we can all agree that murdering daughters is wrong, yes, Malicka, but have you noticed that was never, ever the question?

MALICKA. IT'S ALL TIED UP! This will is saying your girls aren't really yours, they don't belong to your home. It means you don't celebrate when they're born! It's why Punjabi idiots like our fucking father / made us pray for no more girls.

GYAN. Don't say that…

MALICKA. WHAT SHOULD I SAY?! What should I call it, Gyan?

GYAN (*surprised*). Dad was from another time.

MALICKA. NO HE WASN'T. It's 2025 everywhere in the world, *okay*? Including Punjab. This should have stopped by now, it would have stopped three hundred years ago, IF SOMEONE WAS WILLING TO UNDO WHAT THEIR FATHER DID.

GYAN (*looking at* SANGEETA). You don't need to shout.

MALICKA (*to* SANGEETA). You should be standing with us.

You're so trapped!

GYAN. Don't say that she's trapped, Malicka, she doesn't like that.

MALICKA. Can't you see how this affects you too?

SANGEETA. Oh my God! Do you want to know what your problem is?

You three have no idea how to behave around money because you never had any.

MALICKA *flinches*.

MALICKA. You don't understand / because you have had the privilege not to.

SANGEETA. Which is why I'm not getting involved.

MALICKA. Fine. Brilliant. Brilliant. Great. I'm leaving. I'll see you at the conference.

SANGEETA. The conference?!

MALICKA. Yeah.

MALICKA *starts collecting her things*.

SANGEETA. Do not come to the conference. Do not come to the conference.

MALICKA. Why not? I think people there will listen to what we have to say and I think they will care –

MALICKA *stops herself before her voice can betray any emotion.*

(*To* GYAN.) I came, I did everything I could. You heard her.

MALICKA *leaves.*

SANGEETA. If she comes to the conference she is going to look unhinged.

This is not the way to resolve anything.

GYAN. She won't come to the conference, she didn't mean that.

Beat.

When does Angad get back?

SANGEETA. Late. He's canvassing non-stop.

This is what happens if someone doesn't go to a workplace. There's no one to rub against and teach you that your feelings are not facts. Can you imagine believing so entirely in your own version of events?

GYAN. Those two are always at each other's throats, but we'll make sure they sort it before the conference

SANGEETA. Be honest, she's always at his throat.

GYAN. It seems like that but Malicka doesn't let anyone say a word against him. Not even me. I think she's very…

SANGEETA. Self-serving? Dumb?

GYAN. She's upset. She's not explaining herself very well.

I know Angad doesn't like to talk about the past, so maybe you don't understand.

Like, when we were growing up, every day we had to sit at the table until Angad finished his glass of milk.

Malicka used to gulp hers down, but it didn't matter. We couldn't move until Angad finished.

SANGEETA. Those glasses of full-fat milk didn't do Angad any favours.

GYAN. It was confusing.

Dad was this giant in the house, but for some reason all his strength and power was for Angad and we were just there to watch.

Do you see?

Angad mattered, Angad's height mattered, his A levels mattered –

It's really hard to undo that, feeling like the supporting act in your own mind.

SANGEETA. Don't tell me you agree with her?

GYAN. I don't like her threats but… we can all agree, this needs to change.

SANGEETA. So I guess this makes you the good cop.

GYAN. I know Malicka can be hard work but you know this kind of thinking about women isn't right.

SANGEETA. I'm pretty sure she's thinking about cash. Isn't it funny that she became a women's rights activist in the one battle that could win her a property portfolio?

Beat.

GYAN. It really doesn't bother you?

SANGEETA. It bothers me that you two have waited until the worst possible moment to have this conversation.

GYAN. Hang on.

It's not my fault my brother chose the moment my dad died to run for election and erase us from the family.

SANGEETA. You could have brought this up at any point in the last thirty years.

GYAN. But no one ever taps you on the shoulder and says, 'By the way, this is a good moment to talk about how horribly we treat the women in our family.' And whenever you want to say it, there's something else that's more important. Like,

'Shhhhh. If you ask Gandhi what he's doing sleeping naked with his young nieces, you'll make him look creepy and you'll fuck up Independence for everybody so now isn't the time, don't ask him that.'

SANGEETA. What are you talking about?

GYAN. It's funny how it's never a good time for the women's issue, the women just have to suck it up and wait. Do you ever wonder why the women have to suck it up? Why doesn't Gandhi suck it up? Why can't Gandhi just sleep with his wife if he cares so much about Indian Independence? If it's all riding on him and his precious reputation, why doesn't he just put some fucking clothes on?

SANGEETA. Why are you talking about Gandhi?

GYAN. Oh my God, I'm making a point. When is it my moment?

SANGEETA. You sound like a child.

GYAN. Do you think I deserve less than him?

SANGEETA. If your dad thought Angad did more for him. Yeah.

SANGEETA *shrugs. Beat.*

GYAN. Wow.

Malicka's right.

I'm not going to let my little brother, who I dragged up by his shitty little nappies, tell me I'm not my father's child.

SANGEETA. Did Angad say that? Or did your dad say it?

GYAN. Angad is upholding it! He's putting his little fingerprints all over it.

Would this be good enough for you? Would you get over it?

SANGEETA. I honestly think I would and that's what you should be saying to your incredibly privileged, entitled, wealthy sister.

Tell me you'll stop her.

GYAN. Stop her?

Let me put it like this: will this be good enough for your daughter?

SANGEETA....

GYAN. No, of course not. But it's good enough for his sisters, is it?

She starts collecting her stuff to leave.

Malicka's the only one trying to show me something I was too naive and loyal and stupid to even look at.

Why do you think this is good enough for me?

Scene Three

A backstage room at the party conference, at a seaside town in Britain. The decor is dated Regency, high ceilings and flaky paint. There's a trestle table covered with leaflets and lanyards and a catering trolley carrying chocolates, water and sandwiches.

ANGAD *stands on a chair, holding his phone to the window searching for signal.*

PETRA. Why didn't you split it with them?

ANGAD *jumps.*

ANGAD. Sorry. What did you say?

PETRA (*repeating herself*). Why are you sneaking off? You've got a speech in fifteen minutes.

ANGAD *realises he has misheard her.*

ANGAD. I just wanted to make sure my nutso sister hasn't done anything stupid.

PETRA. Oh God, there's one in every family.

ANGAD. I've got two. They got Sangeeta pretty worked up yesterday.

PETRA. Is it just me or are you seriously hot shit this conference?

ANGAD. Do you think so?

PETRA. The party's big dogs are practically queueing to shake your hand.

ANGAD. Lord Fentiman winked at me.

PETRA. I knew a bit of competitive wanking wouldn't hurt you with this party.

ANGAD. It seems like people are really listening to what I've been trying to say. The Shadow Chancellor told me the party and the country need things to change.

That's literally my slogan and he's quoting it to me.

PETRA (*squeals with delight*). Dobson was doing his rapid-fire with the press when I came in and I tell you his face looked like a slapped bottom –

Enter ISAAC.

ISAAC. What are you two doing?

PETRA. Don't look at me like that.

ISAAC. I've been looking everywhere for you.

I've been trying to call you.

ANGAD. Sorry, Isaac, I was hunting for signal.

PETRA. This is how people live in the north.

ANGAD. This is Essex.

PETRA. You know what I mean.

ISAAC. You won't believe what's happened.

ANGAD. Don't tell me my sisters have done / something stupid.

ISAAC. I think Dobson's out.

PETRA. What do you mean?

ISAAC. He's fucking... Ralph Hughes frogmarched him, I think we're actually going to win this.

I need to tell my mum, she's going to lose her shit.

ANGAD. Isaac, please compose yourself. You're not making any sense.

ANGAD holds ISAAC's face, looking him in the eye, trying to calm him down.

What's going on?

ISAAC. Dobson was losing his shit yeah, because none of the big boys turned up to his rapid-fire round and he's there in this half-empty room and everyone's just talking about you yeah.

ANGAD. What are they saying about me?

ISAAC. Honestly, boss, I think they like you.

PETRA. What happened to Dobson?

ISAAC. And you could see Dobson getting more and more annoyed. (*To* PETRA.) And then that girl Alice who went to school with you.

PETRA. Alicia Scholar – *Financial Times* head of bureau, what did she say?

ISAAC. So she asks Dobson how he feels because the whole party is saying they want things to change, and that that's you – that you look and feel and speak like change. And everyone is talking about what it might mean for the party to actually choose a British Indian leader.

That if the party chooses you over Dobson, it shows how much we've changed.

ANGAD. The *FT* said that? They love me! They fucking love me!

PETRA. Focus!

ACT TWO, SCENE THREE 85

ISAAC. And Dobson says. He says, 'Let's be honest. Angad Singh's not really Indian – he had an elite education, he lives in a two-million-pound house. If you heard him on the radio you'd think he was white.'

ANGAD. Can he say that?

PETRA. I thought it still counted.

ANGAD. Me too.

ISAAC. Well, I wasn't sure how people were going to take it because no offence, Angad, you do a whole lot of very white shit.

ANGAD. None taken.

ISAAC. But then before I know it Ralph Hughes is up there on the stage.

PETRA. Talk *faster*, Isaac.

ISAAC. And he takes away the mic.

ANGAD. WHAT DID HE SAY?

ISAAC. And he's like 'Mr Dobson does not represent the view of the party when he suggests that being a person of colour is not compatible with success or prosperity. A person's heritage cannot be taken away from them for their success.' And he apologises to the audience for what Dobson said!

PETRA. You're kidding.

ISAAC. And he takes Dobson by the arm – and bear in mind Dobson doesn't want to leave, he's trying to wriggle out of his grasp – but Ralph Hughes says to him and we all hear it on the mic...

ANGAD. *Yes?*

ISAAC. And he just says it, raw-dog, 'Don't make a scene, Teddy.'

ANGAD *closes his eyes in utter ecstasy at the news.*

And he marches Dobson out of the building.

ANGAD *cheers with his eyes closed in silent celebration.* PETRA *cringes.* ANGAD *starts doing a celebratory dance.*

Is he okay?

PETRA. I think he just needs a minute. Either that or he's having a stroke.

ISAAC. Honestly I felt bad for Dobson. Obviously we all know what he means but you can't be talking like that in 2025.

ANGAD. Am I going to win this thing?

ISAAC. I think you are.

ANGAD. Is this bumfluffed son of a bitch going to be the face of His Majesty's opposition.

ISAAC. I knew it, boss, first time I saw you I knew you were going to the top.

ANGAD. Is this the face?

PETRA. This is the face.

ANGAD. Is this the man?

PETRA. This is the man.

Enter RALPH. *Pause as he watches* ANGAD*'s strange movements.* PETRA *nudges* ANGAD, *who notices* RALPH *and holds out his arms in celebration, as if they might hug.*

ANGAD. Hughesy!

RALPH. Didn't I ask for skeletons to be aired?

Wasn't I clear when I explained that dirty little secrets from your past have a way of coming to the light at the worst possible moment. Maybe I wasn't clear, maybe I owe you an apology? Please, let me know if I there was a breakdown in communication in some way, if there was a problem with my syntax?

ISAAC *holds out a steadying hand.*

ISAAC. I can see you're upset.

ACT TWO, SCENE THREE   87

RALPH. I just got a call from my nephew at *The i* saying Angad's sisters are here at the conference gathering press and before you ask, it's not for a family photo opp.

ANGAD. My sisters are here?

ISAAC. I saw them in the lobby. What's the problem?

RALPH. The problem is Angad's sisters are marching around my conference, telling every journalist who'll listen that they have information / about our leading candidate, that's vital to the public interest, and that's rarely a harbinger of good fucking tidings, is it?

ANGAD. Oh my *God*. Fucking – oh my God. What are they going to say?

RALPH. I don't know, Angad, it doesn't sound good, does it?

So you tell me, / what are they going to say?

ANGAD. I don't know. I don't know!

RALPH. I think you do know or you wouldn't be sweating like a paedophile in a playground right now!

PETRA. Walvis just messaged. Your sisters are going to give a press statement. Opposite the conference

ISAAC. Yeah. Yeah! They're telling everyone here about it.

PETRA *hits* ISAAC*'s arm.*

/ I thought they were canvassing!

RALPH. Fucking hell!

Lights flicker. A discordant hum.

ANGAD. I can't believe they're doing this to me.

RALPH. You can't believe it?

I can't believe you're doing this to *me*.

ANGAD. It's all a mix-up, I've been trying to / clear it up.

RALPH. How did you let it get to this?

ANGAD. I never thought they would do this to me.

RALPH. *Why not?*

Was I not clear? Did I not warn you like an angel from the heavens three days ago: CLEAN YOUR SHITTY CLOSETS. WHY DIDN'T YOU SORT THIS?

ANGAD. BECAUSE EVERYONE KNOWS THE FIRST RULE OF BEING BROWN IS WE DON'T TELL WHITE PEOPLE HOW SHIT WE TREAT EACH OTHER.

Beat.

RALPH (*to* ISAAC). And you. You waved at them, what were you thinking?

ISAAC. I'm sorry, I thought they were here in their capacity as loving family members, not hostile agents of sabotage.

PETRA (*gets a message*). They're giving their press statements in an hour. Right before Angad's speech.

RALPH. FUCK.

What have you done?

ANGAD. It's a misunderstanding.

PETRA. Nothing's gone live yet.

RALPH. What are they going to say, *tell me*.

ANGAD. My sisters are just angry at my dad.

RALPH. Fucking / hell we don't have time for this.

ANGAD. But it's not me, I'm not like that.

ANGAD is about to hear his worst fears. He watches the conversation unfold around him like a nightmare. His anxiety ramps up.

PETRA. This was already a concern in the focus groups.

ANGAD. People said that in our focus groups?

RALPH. 'They have no idea how to behave around money.'

ISAAC. 'Like the cars. So tacky.'

RALPH. So cringe.

PETRA. 'They live with their parents till they're forty but they all drive BMWs.'

ANGAD. Shit. Shit. The voters were worried about that?

RALPH. The women can be quite beautiful but the men are famously unsexy.

ISAAC. Very unsporty.

PETRA. 'Everyone knows they have the smallest penises in the world.'

ANGAD. What?

ISAAC. 'Durex makes a special kind of condom for them.'

PETRA. 'Probably because of colonisation.'

RALPH. 'Probably the tiny dicks.'

ISAAC. 'Must have fucked them up.'

ANGAD puts his head between his knees. PETRA gets a text.

PETRA. Angad's speech is in ten minutes. They're calling him to get mic'd up.

RALPH (*to* PETRA). We need to buy time, delay... speak to the conference organisers. Get Clementine on the stage and tell him to vamp for fifteen.

PETRA. Got it.

PETRA leaves.

RALPH (*to* ISAAC). Seeing as you're on such wonderful, waving terms, why don't you find them both, ideally with a gag in their mouths, for a little family reunion because Angad needs to wipe his arse and make sure it's really clean before he gets up there to do his speech.

ISAAC. Got it. Got it.

ISAAC leaves.

RALPH. No wonder they love dating white men. It's like stepping a hundred years into the future, do you understand me?

ANGAD. What the fuck did you say?

RALPH *taps* ANGAD. *He re-emerges from his cocoon and returns to the room.*

RALPH. When they speak to the press I want to hear what a great brother you are. Do you understand me?

ANGAD. I understand.

RALPH. Is there a way to make this go away?

ANGAD *nods.*

Then do it. Nothing's hit the press, you can nip this in the bud. You were in a good spot at the conference, you're fucking welcome.

It's yours to screw up.

PETRA *re-enters.*

PETRA. I have no idea how to get Paul Clementine on stage. Who would I even speak to about arranging that?

RALPH. Clean this up before your speech, am I clear? Big smiles in the family photograph.

Come on, let's go.

RALPH *leaves with* PETRA.

A moment in the room alone as ANGAD *paces. The moment echoes the time when* ANGAD *was alone in the gurdwara and decided to run. The music, or the lighting.*

ANGAD. *Brilliant.* Are you watching this? Is this what you wanted?

Then why did you do this to me?

ISAAC *shows* MALICKA *and* GYAN *into the room.*

ISAAC. I'll give you all a minute.

ISAAC *flees, leaving the three siblings alone together.*

ACT TWO, SCENE THREE 91

GYAN. You look great, Splinty. That suit is amazing.

ANGAD. Ha. Thanks.

MALICKA. Apparently you have something to say to us?

ANGAD. Yeah. I wasn't expecting to speak about it today but it seems like it can't wait.

MALICKA. / You're right.

GYAN. I didn't want it to happen like this.

ANGAD. It couldn't wait. But it's good to see you two are getting along so well. Right on!

GYAN. You've got something on your –

GYAN licks a tissue and uses it to removes a mark from ANGAD's cheek.

MALICKA. I've always said we should have therapy but no, you two never wanted to talk. This was totally predictable. And avoidable.

MALICKA suddenly grabs the tissue from GYAN's hand and throws it on the floor.

GYAN. *Ow.*

MALICKA. No. He can't sit here, Billy Big Balls, and still need his sister to clean him up. You're not his mother.

GYAN. He's our brother. Angad, I wish it wasn't like this, I know this is an important day for you –

She stops MALICKA from interrupting.

– and we don't want to ruin anything.

We hear you have something to say to us?

ANGAD. I'll do it.

MALICKA. Do what?

ANGAD. I'll do what you want.

MALICKA. We need you to be really, really clear.

ANGAD. I will go against our father's wishes as outlined in his last will and testament. I will distribute his estate in a way that is more acceptable to the two of / you.

MALICKA. Will you make it equal?

ANGAD. I will.

MALICKA. Say it.

ANGAD. I will make it equal.

GYAN *sighs with relief.*

GYAN. I knew you would. I knew you would.

MALICKA. Why?

GYAN *puts out a hand to stop* MALICKA *from speaking. She pulls an envelope out of her handbag.*

GYAN. I can be your witness.

ANGAD. You brought a contract?

MALICKA. 'If it's not in writing then it didn't happen.'

ANGAD *reads the document, laughing bitterly.*

GYAN. It just says that we should each end up with the same.

ANGAD *drags over the trestle table and clears it, in a foul mood.*

ANGAD. Anyone got a pen?

GYAN. Yeah here... We just need a signature and the date on the last page. Here.

MALICKA. Is there anything you want to say?

ANGAD. I have a lot of things I want to say. But I don't think they'd be very helpful.

ANGAD *takes off his pen lid, poised to sign, then stops.*

Is there anything you want to say to me? Sign here '...'

MALICKA. Oh for God's sake.

ANGAD. What?

MALICKA. We're not saying 'please'.

ANGAD. Why not?

GYAN. Come on, let's not turn this into a fight.

ANGAD. You're right. You're at my work with your knives out, warming up the crowds to publicly disembowel me, but we can make it civil.

GYAN. We didn't want it to be like this.

MALICKA. It was your choice to leave it to this.

ANGAD. And I said it, I'll do what you want.

Go on, what do you say?

MALICKA. We aren't going to grovel.

ANGAD. I'm not asking you to grovel, I'm asking for manners.

GYAN. I can't say 'please'.

ANGAD. Why not?

GYAN. Because I need you to believe that sharing it is the right thing. I need you to believe it's ours as much as it's yours.

ANGAD. You want me to say, two plus two equals five. Don't just say it, believe it.

GYAN. If you sign it, we can move on.

ANGAD. Ask me nicely and I'll sign it.

MALICKA. We aren't going to kowtow to you as if you're doing us a favour.

ANGAD. This isn't a six-figure favour?

GYAN. Don't make this about the money.

ANGAD. It's literally about money, my money, so be nice to me.

GYAN. I AM NICE TO YOU. I collected you from school. I taught you how to brush your teeth. And I never once got a 'please', or a 'thank you', or even 'are you okay?'

ANGAD. Come on – I'm sharing this out of my good grace, I don't owe you anything, so the least you can do is show a little class while you fuck me. In the *arse*. On the most important day of my career.

MALICKA. Sign it, or I'm going out there and telling this entire conference exactly what you're doing.

ANGAD. What am I doing?

GYAN. You know, Angad, please don't pretend you don't.

ANGAD. What have I actually done?

MALICKA. You saw how we were invisible in that house. I'll tell them / how you let us wait on you, hand and foot –

ANGAD. Oh I bet they'll love that –

MALICKA. You could use your platform to do the right thing, but you don't want to –

ANGAD. 'Disgusting brown man oppresses his women' fucking *lovely*.

GYAN. If you were the man you've been saying you are, you'd be the first one to tear up Dad's will.

MALICKA. And maybe they can forgive it in a seventy-eight-year-old man born in rural Punjab in the 1940s, but it will not be forgiven from you.

ANGAD. I'm not Dad.

MALICKA. Prove it!

MALICKA *takes* ANGAD's *hand and starts to force him to sign the paper.*

ANGAD. What are you doing?... Get off me.

MALICKA. Just sign it!

ANGAD *shakes* MALICKA *off and backs away from her.*
MALICKA *holds on to the contract.*

ANGAD. First nice thing my dad ever did for me and you want me to throw it away.

MALICKA. Pathetic.

The only one mentioned in Dad's will, complaining about how hard he had it.

GYAN. We can't move on until you're ready to be honest about what we went through.

ANGAD. You want honesty? Well, you can start by being honest about yourself.

ANGAD *starts throwing sandwiches at* GYAN.

I'll start: Gyan, course you need the money. You can't send your kids to state school.

GYAN *lunges for* ANGAD *but he escapes her.*

GYAN. Don't you dare talk about my boys.

ANGAD. They are thick as two planks, they need every leg up you can give them. Just be honest about it. And you – (*To* MALICKA.) I feel bad for you, I really do.

How can you hide your Botox from your husband if he's the one who's paying for it?

MALICKA. I do not have Botox.

ANGAD. Yes you do!

GYAN *and* MALICKA *pin* ANGAD *down. He struggles against them.*

MALICKA. Pathetic.

ANGAD. Hey! Hey, stop that.

MALICKA. I do not have Botox. *Say it.*

ANGAD. You do! I can see it! / Why can't you smile?

MALICKA. Dad's will is disgusting. Say it.

ANGAD. It's what he wanted.

Stop it! Get off me! I can't – I can't… Hey stop it.

ANGAD *keeps trying to catch his breath. He can't.*

MALICKA. Now you say 'please'.

>GYAN *takes* ANGAD's *hand, and tries to force a signature.*

ANGAD (*gasping*). FUCKING GET OFF ME.

GYAN. How does it feel to be on the bottom?

MALICKA. ARE YOU GOING TO SIGN IT OR NOT?

GYAN. He'll sign it. He's going to do what we say.

>ANGAD *screams with utter rage and throws them off him.*

ANGAD. GET THE FUCK OFF ME.

>GYAN *and* MALICKA *survey him, slightly sheepish. That went too far.* ANGAD *is coughing, and spluttering, furious, red-faced.*

GYAN. Angad...

ANGAD. DON'T FUCKING TOUCH ME

>ANGAD *starts tearing the contract.*

MALICKA. I guess there's nothing left to say. There's a lot of people out there who want to hear / about this.

>MALICKA *goes to collect her bag.* ANGAD *blocks her.*

ANGAD. SHUT THE FUCK UP AND LISTEN TO ME!

GYAN. Angad... Let's try and take the heat out of this –

ANGAD. You better tell them that I was working in the shops, driving to Spitalfields at four a.m. to get vegetables. I took out loans for him, I graduated with fifty K of his debts that I'm still paying off because my money was his money. Do you remember that, Malicka? Our little memory-keeper, did you tell your therapist that?

MALICKA. I don't have to listen to this. Get out of my way.

ANGAD. *Yes you do.* Today you're going to listen to me. For *once*. That man choked me my whole life. But you don't see that. You don't see anything unless it smacks you in the head.

Do you? Do you need me to smack you in the head for you to wake up?

He makes a pretend gesture of punching MALICKA *and she flinches. He laughs.*

Wakey wakey!

GYAN. Angad...

ANGAD. You two got out. You got married and he stopped owning you. You have the space to laugh about him and get therapy about him because he wasn't choking you till the day he died.

The hoover is a funny story for you but I lived it – the hoover, the belt, the hockey stick, and you never wanted the same as me then, do you remember? Don't you remember?

He grabs MALICKA *by the ear and pulls her down to the floor.*

Remember this one.

GYAN. Angad, let go of her.

ANGAD. Will you tell them that he did this to me? And he never did it to you.

Will you tell them that he tied me up?

Will you tell them you never wanted half of this?

MALICKA. Get off me.

GYAN. Angad. Stop. You need to stop now.

ANGAD. You do not have the monopoly on being a victim. / Say it.

MALICKA. Angad.

ANGAD. SAY IT.

MALICKA (*still with tons of attitude*). I don't have the monopoly on being a victim.

GYAN. Listen to me right now. STOP THIS.

ANGAD. He gave it to me, because I earned it.

He twists her ear.

MALICKA. Aaah!

GYAN. Get off her!

ANGAD. I should have done this years ago. Say it.

MALICKA. You earned it.

ANGAD. Say it again.

MALICKA. You earned it.

ANGAD. Say it till you mean it, you stupid fucking bitch.

ANGAD lets go of her ear and pushes her away from himself. MALICKA *stays on the floor, horrified.*

I would have killed to be invisible in that house and you know it.

Every day I'd wake up and hope that he had died. He fucking ruined my life, and now you two are carrying on his good work. Tell them what you want, I don't give a shit any more, I just want to be free from you lot.

MALICKA *reaches for her bag from the floor.* ANGAD *grabs it from* MALICKA, *drops it on his foot, kicking the contents out flying.*

Sayonara, you cunts. Now get lost.

MALICKA *furiously crawls on the floor, picking up her stuff.* SANGEETA *enters and stares the scene unfolding around her.*

GYAN. So that's a 'no'?

SANGEETA *starts to help* MALICKA.

SANGEETA. Are you okay?

MALICKA. I don't need your help. Leave me alone.

Pause.

GYAN *watches* ANGAD.

MALICKA *has finished collecting her stuff, head down, she tries to leave.*

Just leave him, Gyan. Please, let's go.

Seeing that GYAN *intends to talk further,* MALICKA *walks away.*

GYAN. You know what you really learned in that school. How to pretend to be something you're not. How didn't I see it before? You got so good at hiding who you are that I didn't even notice. You look like him. You think like him and you act like him, you're just wrapped up in an expensive suit and a very expensive accent.

ANGAD. Good. Now fuck off.

GYAN. You're lost.

GYAN *leaves.*

SANGEETA. What the hell was that?

ANGAD. What?

SANGEETA. What were you doing to her?

ANGAD. I was sticking up for myself like you always wanted. Are you happy? Let me guess. No.

SANGEETA. Did you sort things out?

ANGAD. Yes.

SANGEETA. And? Are they going to talk to the press?

ANGAD. Sounds like it.

SANGEETA. So you didn't sort it. What are they going to say?

ANGAD *makes a flippant gesture: 'No idea.'*

Why didn't you sort it?

ANGAD. I realised, they never said 'please'. Not once. They said 'fuck you' plenty of times. They wanted to take my money and still call me a piece of shit?

Nah. Nah. Nah.

SANGEETA. Angad, what's got into you? Why are you talking like this?

ANGAD. They lost this election for me. They fucked me. I could've made history.

SANGEETA. What just happened?

ANGAD. Nothing.

SANGEETA. She was crying, Angad! She was terrified.

ANGAD. Malicka's a good actress.

SANGEETA. Let me guess, she was making it up? Who else used to say that?

Beat.

ANGAD. What about me? What about what they did to me?

SANGEETA. What did they do?

ANGAD. Threatening me! Controlling me! Ruining my life just like my fucking dad.

SANGEETA. You can't blame this one on your dad.

ANGAD. Telling me he broke his back SO THAT I...

And then he ruins it, he fucking ruins everything. Nothing can ever make it right... But now I can finally breathe.

SANGEETA. The only thing your dad did today was fuck you up so much your whole life that you think behaving like an illiterate Southall thug is the way to get what you want, acting like a deranged animal at the most public moment of your career, thirty minutes before you're supposed to give a speech!

I'm sorry, Angad, but you're not cut out for politics, and it's not because you're imprecise or self-serving or balding – you're actually too fucked up.

ANGAD. Wow.

SANGEETA. I don't recognise you. I didn't marry the rich guy, or the smart guy, or the handsome guy. I married the good guy.

ANGAD. I am the good guy!

ANGAD *tries to get closer to* SANGEETA; *he puts a hand on her stomach. She flinches away.*

Alright, Sangeeta. Thank you. Thank you for your good wishes.

Now if you'll excuse me, I just want a moment to myself before I go out there for my public mauling. Thank you.

SANGEETA. You are feral and starving and ungenerous to your soul and you need to stop.

ANGAD. I don't think I can say it any clearer: CAN YOU FUCK. OFF.

SANGEETA *covers her face.*

Oh wow, now you're crying. Let me guess? After everything you just said, I'm the arsehole.

SANGEETA *can't compose herself.*

Give me a break.

SANGEETA *wipes her face and looks at him.* ANGAD *stares back at her.* SANGEETA *shakes her head.*

SANGEETA. This isn't the man I married.

SANGEETA *leaves in disbelief.*

ANGAD *closes the door, then opens it and closes it again. He bangs the door repeatedly.*

ANGAD *starts to kick over furniture. He tears the contract up further. The scene culminates with him banging his head as the stage goes dark.*

Scene Four

One hour later. Backstage at the party conference. The stage is prepared for Angad's speech. PETRA *scrolls through her phone, reading frantically.*

PETRA. It's bad, Isaac.

ISAAC. I know.

PETRA. It's really, really bad.

ISAAC. I know, I was there, I watched them do it live and I just thought, damn. Angad is such a little bitch.

PETRA. It's going down like cold sick with the press.

ISAAC. Ralph Hughes tried to do some damage control but no one was buying it.

PETRA. No. Course they weren't.

ISAAC. Angad said it was just a misunderstanding. I thought he was going to fix it.

PETRA *shows* ISAAC *her phone.*

PETRA. Do you think that's true?

ISAAC. Honestly, I have no idea.

PETRA. I thought these stories about ethnic minorities oppressing their women were racist propaganda.

ISAAC. What the hell do I know?

PETRA. Why didn't he split it with them?

ISAAC. I don't know. It seems like a really easy way to be the good guy.

PETRA *puts her phone away.*

PETRA. I actually can't read it. Fucking arsehole. Have you seen him since this broke?

ISAAC *shakes his head and looks at the time.*

ISAAC. Have you?

PETRA. Not a peep. We can't delay his speech any longer.

ISAAC. Do you think we should go out and say he isn't coming? We can announce he's withdrawing from the contest and finish this.

PETRA. We can't say it for him.

PETRA drops her voice.

We need to distance ourselves from him. Visibly.

ISAAC. Tell me about it. I did an assembly at my old school about working for him. This is so fucking embarrassing.

PETRA. All afternoon, when people ask me where he is, I've just been saying, 'No idea, haven't spoken to him.' I'm not explicitly saying I quit months ago, but I'm trying to incept the thought that I might have quit months ago.

ISAAC. I threw my badge in the toilet, checking no one was watching, like it was a fucking baggie.

PETRA. You've only been with him for six months you can just write this off your CV. I've got four years tied up with him and I need to make it clear that I'm as shocked and appalled as everyone else who's heard this. I need to do it before he loses.

ANGAD appears, dishevelled with blood on his face.

ISAAC. Angad.

PETRA. What are you doing?

ANGAD. It's time for my speech.

ISAAC and PETRA exchange a glance.

ANGAD. What?...What is it?

PETRA. You've got a little...

PETRA points to the corner of his mouth. ANGAD wipes his lip.

ANGAD. How about now?

PETRA. Good. Gone.

> ANGAD *still looks terrible.*

ANGAD. How's my tie?

PETRA. It's fine.

ANGAD. Let's do the concealer then.

PETRA. I have some bad news.

> PETRA *starts reluctantly applying his concealer.*
>
> Your sisters have given a rather devastating statement to the press.
>
> You come across very poorly.
>
> You come across like a slimy hypocrite who doesn't believe a word of his own manifesto.
>
> PETRA *finishes, and involuntarily wipes her hand on her leg.*

ANGAD. Don't be so dramatic.

> *Beat.* PETRA *laughs, incredulous. Angry.*

PETRA. I'm not.

> PETRA *shows* ANGAD *reams of messages on her phone.*
>
> All since the release, all withdrawing their offers of support, or their pledges to your election fund. This is a big deal. I think you need to resign.
>
> *Beat.*
>
> You can relaunch in 2029, if that's what you want.

ANGAD. What about you, Isaac, what do you think?

ISAAC. About what?

ANGAD. About the weather.

> Will Arsenal win the Premier League?
>
> What do you think 'about what'? Do you think I have to resign?

ISAAC. I heard their press release, Angad. It didn't feel good to be working for you. What you've done is embarrassing.

ANGAD. Let me tell you something I wish I knew, Isaac.

We're allowed to be ambitious.

We're allowed to like money.

We're allowed to want power.

ISAAC. You said you were better, but you're not. You're just the same.

ANGAD. We don't have to be better than them to do the same job.

ISAAC. You're not going to change anything.

ANGAD. Hypocritical white men have been doing this job for four hundred years and if I'd won this, you better believe something would have changed.

ISAAC. I've decided to accept a job on Edward Dobson's team.

ANGAD *laughs*.

PETRA. *What?*

ISAAC. I don't want it to be awkward. At least I know what Dobson stands for.

PETRA. How the hell did you swing that?

ISAAC. We have mutual friends.

ANGAD. Good to see you getting grubby with the grown-ups, Isaac.

ANGAD *looks at the stage where he's about to speak, psyching himself up for his imminent speech.*

PETRA. How do you have mutual friends with Edward Dobson?

ISAAC. He went to my school.

PETRA. He was at Westminster.

ISAAC *shrugs: 'So?'*

But you're on the diversity access scheme.

ISAAC. I am diverse.

PETRA. I can't believe this.

ISAAC. I WAS A DAY BOY.

ANGAD. Brilliant. Thanks, team.

ANGAD starts to walk onto the stage. RALPH *enters, and intercepts him.*

RALPH. No way.

ANGAD. Excuse me.

RALPH. No fucking way, you are not showing this face at my conference.

I don't want to hear your speech, I don't want to hear your excuses YOU ARE NOT SPEAKING HERE. You called yourself progress and change / and Christ it's embarrassing to even –

ANGAD. You're going to tell me what change looks like?

RALPH. No chance, do not play the brown card with me, you are talking to the bloody maharaja of spin. I know when I see sexism, misogyny and blatant discrimination and trust me, our voters will know it too.

Jesus Christ, what were you thinking?

ANGAD. Hypocritical white men have been / doing this job –

RALPH. *No.* Don't even try it. Your strategy is apologise, apologise fast, do it a lot, then don't show your face in Westminster for a while.

Not here – (*Referring to how terrible* ANGAD *looks.*) I'll announce your resignation to this lot, apologise on your own time.

ANGAD. Guess I'm not cut out for public office.

ACT TWO, SCENE FOUR   107

RALPH. Yup, all of you, *Westminster Hour* is over for you / lot.

PETRA. I am as shocked and appalled as everyone else who's heard / this –

ISAAC. I don't work for / him any more.

RALPH. Shut up. No. That's it. I'm ending this now.

RALPH walks onto the stage and addresses the conference from the podium. PETRA *starts to pace – her career is over too?*

ANGAD. Well, that's it, team. Too fucked up for public office.

RALPH. Good afternoon, party conference.

I know I am not on the agenda, but Mr Singh will not be speaking today. There is no denying that the recent scrutiny and public concern surrounding his conduct has made it difficult for him to continue in the leadership contest. Mr Singh recognises the distraction this has caused and I have accepted his resignation from the contest.

ANGAD *walks onto the stage. He has cleaned up. He approaches the podium.*

Mr Singh brought ambition and a bold vision to the party, ideas that sparked genuine hope for progress, and this will not be forgotten.

And now to say a few words of apology himself is Mr Singh... Very briefly.

ANGAD. Sorry, sorry to interrupt... sorry. Hello. Good afternoon, party conference.

Beat.

Mr Hughes would like me to apologise...

Beat. ANGAD *looks out and considers the mass of the conference.*

Sorry, what am I apologising for?

RALPH. Well. I imagine –

ANGAD. Am I apologising for my father? For my family? For where I come from?

RALPH. I think our members today expect an apology for the way you have treated the women / in your family –

ANGAD. I thought we lived in Great Britain, a diverse, multicultural nation, I thought that was the great strength of this nation.

RALPH. No one is questioning multiculturalism here –

ANGAD. I thought that in Great Britain, individuals are free to work hard, raise their families and that the / wishes of the deceased –

RALPH. That is not under question, / party conference.

ANGAD. Can I finish?

I thought the state can't tell you how you spend your money, or distribute your assets, so long as you aren't breaking the law.

RALPH. Mr Singh, you've sat on the Select Committee for gender inequality – surely / your conduct –

PETRA *shouts over from the audience.*

PETRA. Excuse me, Mr Hughes. Did your mother get her father's title? What's your father's plan for his estate when he dies?

RALPH. What?

RALPH *gestures to the wings for security to deal with this.*

PETRA. Surely I don't have to explain primogeniture to you.

RALPH. Well, this is entirely different –

PETRA. Do hereditary peerages in the Lords pass down to women? No. Can I just be absolutely clear: have you ever objected to that?

RALPH (*offside*). Can we get / someone to…

ACT TWO, SCENE FOUR   109

PETRA. What happens to estates in your family?

ANGAD. Yes exactly. In my culture, women get a dowry. We have an ancient system to protect them and give them independent wealth, outside of inheritance. Did you know that?

ISAAC *covers his face.*

RALPH. Well. No, Mr Singh, I must confess my ignorance –

ANGAD. When I decided to run for election I expected to defend my campaign promises, my manifesto, my agenda.

I did not expect to stand here as a proud Anglo-Sikh man to defend tolerance.

RALPH. Well, yes, I'm sorry – I actually hadn't realised there was a cultural aspect to all of this –

ANGAD. These are practices which frankly, you should educate yourself on before you comment.

RALPH. I apologise. I will educate myself.

ANGAD. We're used to this.

Mr Hughes wants me to apologise. He doesn't like my father's will?

Let me make it absolutely clear:

I kept it. Because I earnt it.
I kept it. Because I worked my whole life for it.
I kept it. Because it's mine.

I said I had clawed my way from the bottom;
I said I knew what it was to struggle.
I said I'd had to fight for what I'd earnt.

Did I say it made me selfless?
Did I say it made me soft?
Did I say it was to give it away?

You.
Why do you stay late at work?
Why do you try so hard?

Do you do it so you can give it away?
Or do you want life, your life, your kid's life to get better.

I thought so.

Right? So we're all on the same page?

He says I should be sorry.
But he doesn't know, because he's never been HUNGRY.
Mr Hughes didn't crawl from the bottom.
He didn't have to fight for every penny.
AND THIS IS WHAT IT LOOKS LIKE.

The party liked my story. The voters want to believe my story. I'm still telling the same story. I AM EXACTLY WHO I SAID I WAS:

I am the son of a baggage handler, who came here with three pounds in his pocket. THIS IS WHAT IT LOOKS LIKE.

I am a man who knows what it is to struggle. THIS IS WHAT IT LOOKS LIKE.

I am a man who's had to fight every inch, to get to where he is.

Not to give it away. For life to get better. For *my life* to get better.

Should I apologise? BECAUSE THIS. IS. WHAT. IT LOOKS LIKE.

He steps down from the podium, buzzing with adrenaline.
He slowly comes down to earth. The crowd is cheering.
PETRA *adjusts his tie.*

MALICKA (*from the crowd*). HYPOCRITE.

MALICKA *leaves the auditorium.*

PETRA. I know exactly how to play this.

ANGAD. Do you now?

PETRA *nods, smiling out at the crowd.*

Do you think they liked that?

ACT TWO, SCENE FOUR 111

PETRA. Well, they're still cheering.

ISAAC. It's looking pretty divisive.

ANGAD. In a good way?

PETRA. Was that good, what I said to Ralph?

ANGAD. Very good.

RALPH *approaches* ANGAD.

RALPH (*aside*). About before, I'm not too proud to admit… there may have been some unconscious bias at play.

ISAAC. Mixed reactions on X… Some people fucking love it.

RALPH *proffers a hand for* ANGAD *to shake*.

PETRA. I think this lot liked it… Can we get some photos over here!

PETRA *puts her arms around* ANGAD *and kisses his cheek. The flash of a photograph being taken.*

ANGAD. I want to celebrate. We should all be celebrating.

ISAAC *lingers on the outside, awkwardly declining the photographers' offers to photograph him with the victorious gang.*

PETRA *brings champagne.*

Where are my girls?

PETRA *spots* SANGEETA *in the crowd and brings her up on the stage.* ANGAD *puts his arm around* SANGEETA.

SANGEETA. Angad. That was –

A camera flashes.

ANGAD. Smile, baby.

SANGEETA *takes a sip of champagne and then runs off to vomit in a bucket. She wipes her mouth and decides to return. She puts on a strained smile.*

ISAAC *spots* GYAN *by an exit. He tries to ask her to come on stage.*

GYAN. Why are they cheering?

ISAAC. This is a big moment. You're going to want a photo.

GYAN. You really don't care, do you? It's all talk.

GYAN *runs out of the auditorium.*

ANGAD. Where are my girls?

PETRA *and* RALPH *position* ANGAD *for pictures.* SANGEETA *is there, but practically recoiling.*

(*Looking for* SANGEETA.) What do you think, do you think that was good?

SANGEETA *is still smiling, strained, into the audience. She waves to* ANGAD *but ignores his gesture that she should come to his side.*

PETRA. The camera is this way. Angad, what's that in your hair?

She tidies him up.

ANGAD. Does this champagne smell weird?

PETRA. Nah, it smells great.

ANGAD. I think it was corked.

PETRA. It tastes like victory.

ANGAD *continues posing for photos flanked by* PETRA *and* RALPH.

SANGEETA *continues to recoil from* ANGAD, *and avoids him whilst being on stage.*

ISAAC *is on the sidelines, looking at what he missed out on. Clapping to the music, filled with regret.*

Three long pieces of confetti fall from the sky, marking the end of the conference.

Epilogue

Three months later. SANGEETA *and* GYAN *stand in the living room of the Singh household. It seems more stark.*

SANGEETA. Everything's really good. Thank you.

GYAN. Was it a natural birth?

SANGEETA. No.

GYAN. Thank you for seeing me.

SANGEETA. You said you have something you wanted to say?

GYAN. I do... I do.

Beat.

I guess it's really for Angad. Is he here?

SANGEETA (*shaking her head*). He's so busy right now.

GYAN. Yeah. Course. I got her something.

GYAN *takes out a little red velvet pouch, typical of Indian jewellers. When* SANGEETA *does not take it,* GYAN *opens it herself. Inside is a tiny golden kara* (*the bracelet all Sikhs wear*).

Mum and Dad bought them for my boys when they were born. If they were around they would have got her one and I didn't know if... obviously no one in your family is Sikh so. I thought she might not have one.

She'll always remember her bhua got her her first one.

SANGEETA. You shouldn't have.

GYAN. You can't say 'no' to a kara. Really, you can't. Here. Take it.

SANGEETA *reluctantly accepts the box.*

SANGEETA. How's Malicka?

GYAN. Malicka? I haven't really heard much from her since she went back.

Beat.

I've been trying to keep busy.

I went to Southall on the weekend. The boys were with their dad and I just realised, I'll probably never have a reason to go there again.

I used to love going to the Broadway with Dad. He'd wear that leather jacket with his bumbag of cash, strapped across his chest and people would come out the shops just to shake his hand.

Man of the people. Angad got that from him.

SANGEETA. That's good, Gyan.

GYAN. With everything that happened we didn't really get a chance to be sad together. It was easier to feel angry than sad…

I guess Angad thought it was easier to run for election than feel sad.

And now, I guess that's passed.

SANGEETA. That sounds good.

Beat.

GYAN. Um. I –

I've been, um, I've been thinking about where Dad came from, the stuff he saw.

Like Punjab in the 1940s, what he saw and what that maybe did to him?

I guess he had to see a lot of people who weren't going to make it and he just had to keep going and not stop.

I think that does something to you. Knowing you might not make it.

Does Angad ever talk about that?

SANGEETA. Angad can't keep raking over the past.

You said there was something you wanted to say.

GYAN. I've been thinking about Angad's speech. The speech he gave at the gurdwara.

That he wanted things to get better.

I think I really believed that. I wanted it too, I wanted it to happen faster.

Do you know what I mean?

SANGEETA. I think I'm not the right person to hear this.

GYAN. I know you think things were never good between us. But you're wrong.

We've always had this kind of...

She makes a gesture of butting heads.

We're close, but we need to get things out.

SANGEETA. Okay.

GYAN. It didn't mean –

Everything that happened, it doesn't mean we don't love each other.

You get that, you have a brother.

SANGEETA. I do have a brother. But I can't imagine a world where I do what you did, where I try to hurt him.

I can't imagine a world where I'm not in Isher's corner.

GYAN. Okay yeah, fine but – why?

Don't you ask yourself, like, why is that?!

Beat.

It's not because you're better than us.

It's not because you love your brother more.

It's because you weren't pitted against each other. If I were you I would feel lucky that my parents didn't do this to me, you're lucky, Sangeeta, you're not better than us.

SANGEETA. Okay. Whatever you say.

Is there anything else?

GYAN. Help us to get through this.

SANGEETA. I can't fix this for you, Gyan.

The relationship contract is the relationship contract, Gyan, and what you did...

That was your choice.

GYAN. But that's not everything, Sangeeta. We – I remember when he was born.

Through the baby monitor, a baby starts to fuss and whimper. SANGEETA *switches off the monitor.*

That matters.

Is that her?

SANGEETA. I should go.

GYAN. What's her name?

SANGEETA. You've said what you needed to say.

GYAN. Please, Sangeeta, for Angad's sake.

Help us get past this. You have to help us.

SANGEETA. You did this.

GYAN. I was grieving for my dad. Angad is too.

Angad needs people in his life who understand him.

SANGEETA. He has me.

GYAN. You grew up in Chiswick! Your dad buys your mum flowers.

We need people who understand where we came from.

There was a lot of love on top of those shops and I can't let him forget that.

SANGEETA. But you wanted this, you chose it.

You held a gun to his head and pulled the trigger.

GYAN. But it didn't matter!

He won the leadership, we can get past it.

SANGEETA. But he knows you tried to hurt him, and he can't go back from there.

You see that, don't you?

GYAN. Angad needs me, / I need him –

SANGEETA. He needs people he can trust.

GYAN. No one else will ever understand.

Will you please tell him I came today?

SANGEETA *laughs*.

SANGEETA. You think he doesn't know you're here?

GYAN. He knows –

The sound of a baby crying starts; not through the monitor from upstairs.

SANGEETA. You think it's me, telling him what to do, keeping you away from him?

GYAN. He needs me.

SANGEETA. He doesn't want to see you.

GYAN. Can I meet her?

SANGEETA. I'm sorry.

GYAN. Just this once.

SANGEETA. He made me promise I wouldn't let you see her.

GYAN. No he didn't.

SANGEETA. He did.

GYAN. Please. We have to get through this.

SANNGEETA. Sometimes, Gyan, there are catastrophic accidents and hundreds of tonnes of chemical waste get poured into the ocean. And they can't be taken out again.

The baby's cry gets louder.

GYAN. I wanted things to change.

SANGEETA. I know.

GYAN. I remember when he was born.

SANGEETA. I have to go. I'll show you out.

The walls fall away. We move through the house to a liminal space where baby Avneen is crying (Lindo Wing, two months, name down for Bute House).

ANGAD *enters.*

ANGAD. Hey, what's wrong?

The crying continues.

Don't cry, Daddy's here.

If anything, the cry gets louder. He picks her up.

Hey, shhhhh. It's okay, Daddy's here.

ANGAD *tries to soothe his wailing daughter, but she does not stop.*

Daddy's here. Why are you crying?

End of play.

Acknowledgements

This play first lived at a Tamasha scratch night in 2019; it then had a reading at Park Theatre in 2021, made possible by the Prism Project. Thank you to these amazing companies for making space for it.

I want to thank Nina Steiger, the head of play development at the NT Studio, who came to this early reading of *The Estate* and first saw its potential. Her words have echoed in my mind like mantras throughout its five-year development, encouraging me to be bolder.

The National Theatre Studio allowed me to dream and re-dream this play over years. I want to thank everyone there who made writing feel playful, supported and never lonely – I won't list names for fear of omissions and inevitable social anxiety. I am especially grateful to the wonderful dramaturgs there who I have leaned on throughout, first Stewart Pringle and then Jeanie O'Hare and, of course, Nina.

A huge thank-you to Rufus Norris for his decision to programme this play, and to Indhu Rubasingham who supported its development and rehearsals. They have made the National a place where stories can be complicated, messy and ugly, when they want to be.

Thank you to my friend Dan for agreeing to direct this play, and turning it into something I couldn't imagine.

To the incredibly talented cast, Adeel, Dinita, Fode, Helena, Humphrey, Shelley and Thusitha: it is a wonderful feeling to be surprised, hearing words you've written.

To the absolutely stacked creative team: Chloe, Khadija, Asaf, Mike, Bryony, Alex, Polly, Shereen, Molly and Jessica who brought their genius to this project and turned it into a show.

To the unwavering diligence of the stage management team: the first ones in and last ones out every day, Ian, Lizzie, Aida and Tracey. A huge thank-you.

I owe great thanks to my brother, Isher, for taking my idea to write a play in my last year of medical school seriously and for giving me vital advice that I still refer to.

To Jaskaran who read a first draft of this play in 2018 and told me 'this play will be on at the National Theatre' at a time when it was absurd.

To my husband Shubham Saraf who showed me I should lean on the genius of actors. Who taught me how to write arguments where no one listens and no one understands why they're upset. Who stays up late thinking of my problems.

To my mother Kulwant, who took me to the theatre to see *The Mousetrap* three times and limited my screen time to make me write stories.

To my father Onkar, who allowed me to watch ten hours of television a day all summer. And of whom I have never been afraid (I finally see that's because of his strength, not mine).

And to my fearless Baba from whom I inherited my best qualities.

S.S.